GRAMMAR LAND

Grammar in Fun for the Children of
Schoolroom Shire

Grammar Land: Grammar in Fun for the Children of Schoolroom Shire (Annotated)
By M. L. Nesbitt

Originally published in 1878 by Henry Holt and Company: New York
This work is in the public domain.

Edited and annotated by Amy M. Edwards and Christina J. Mugglin © 2018.

Published by Blue Sky Daisies
Wichita, Kansas
blueskydaisies.wordpress.com

Cover design © 2018 by Blue Sky Daisies.

ISBN-13: 978-1-944435-04-2
ISBN-10: 1-944435-04-2

Grammar in Fun for the Children of Schoolroom Shire

By M. L. Nesbitt

Updated with Worksheets and Answer Key

Edited by Amy M. Edwards and Christina J. Mugglin

Originally published in 1878 by Henry Holt and Company: New York

Updated 2018 edition by Blue Sky Daisies

BLUE SKY DAISIES

Publishing Books Old and New

Other titles by Blue Sky Daisies:

Geography Books
*Elementary Geography by Charlotte Mason
*Home Geography for Primary Grades with Written and Oral Exercises by C. C. Long

Language Arts and Grammar Books
*The Mother Tongue: Adapted for Modern Students by George Lyman Kittredge
    In this series: Workbook 1 and 2; Answer Key 1 and 2
Exercises in Dictation by F. Peel

The CopyWorkBook Series
The CopyWorkBook: George Washington's Rules of Civility & Decent Behavior in Company and Conversation by Amy M. Edwards and Christina J. Mugglin

Other Titles
The Birds' Christmas Carol by Kate Douglas Wiggin
The Innkeeper's Daughter by Michelle Lallement
Kipling's Rikki-Tikki-Tavi: A Children's Play by Amy M. Edwards

*Like *Grammar Land*, these titles are popular with those inspired by Charlotte Mason and her educational philosophy.

About This Edition

Blue Sky Daisies is pleased to bring you this annotated edition of the classic title *Grammar Land: Grammar in Fun for the Children of Schoolroom Shire*. The original text of the 1878 book is faithfully reproduced, but completely retypeset for a pleasant reading experience.

We have also taken the grammar exercises suggested in the original text and developed convenient worksheets for completing those exercises. Furthermore, an answer key is included in the back of this book. Both the worksheets and the answer key may be copied for your home use only.

The Editors
Amy M. Edwards
Christina J. Mugglin
2018

Preface

Grammar Land

The favorable reception that the former editions of this little book have met with, calls for a word of acknowledgment. It seems that not only the little folks for whom it was intended, but children of a larger growth have read it with interest; and students, who spend days and nights "with weary eyesight poring over miserable books," have condescended to turn over these pages, and laughingly admit that the imagination may sow even the dustiest of bookshelves with flowers.

Teachers of the younger classes in schools have found this little volume extremely useful; and it is suggested, that though children will often read it with pleasure by themselves, they will derive much more profit from it when it is made the textbook for a lesson. The simple exercises appended to each chapter will then be found both useful and entertaining.

Third Edition, 1878

To all little children who think grammar hard and dry, this book is dedicated, by one who loves to see sunshine in Schoolroom Shire.

Contents

Grammar Land Worksheets

Introduction
Judge Grammar and His Subjects

WHAT is Grammar Land? Where is Grammar Land? Have you ever been to Grammar Land? Wait a minute and you shall hear. You will not find Grammar Land marked on the globe, and I never saw a map of it; but then, who ever saw a map of Fairyland? and yet you have all heard of that, and know a great deal about it, of course. Well, Grammar Land is a place every bit as real as Fairyland, and much more important. The Fairy Queen is all very well, and a very great little queen in her way; but Judge Grammar! great, stern, old Judge Grammar, is far mightier than any Fairy Queen, for he rules over real kings and queens down here in Matter-of-fact-land. Our kings and queens, and emperors too, have all to obey Judge Grammar's laws, or else they would talk what is called *bad grammar*; and then, even their own subjects would laugh at them, and would say: "Poor things! When they were children, and lived in Schoolroom Shire, they can never have been taken to Grammar Land! How shocking!" And Judge Grammar himself—well, I cannot say what he would do, as I suppose such a thing never really happened; for who could imagine a king or queen saying, *"I is,"* or *"you was,"* or *"it wasn't me."* No one speaks in that way except people who have never heard of Judge Grammar.

Ah! I wish you could see him—this great Judge—sitting on his throne in his court, and giving orders about his precious words, which are the riches of Grammar Land. For Judge Grammar says that all the words that you can say belong really to him, and he can do what he likes with them; he is, in fact, King as well as Judge over Grammar Land. Now, you know that when William the Conqueror conquered England he divided the land among his nobles, and they had it for their own so long as they obeyed the king and helped him in his wars. It was just the same with Judge Grammar when he took possession of Grammar Land; he gave all the words to his nine followers, to take for their very own as long as they obeyed him. These nine followers he called the nine Parts-of-Speech, and to one or other of them every word in Grammar Land was given.

They are funny fellows, these nine Parts-of-Speech. You will find out by-and-by which you like best amongst them all. There is rich Mr. Noun, and his useful friend Pronoun; little ragged Article, and talkative Adjective; busy Dr. Verb, and Adverb; perky Preposition, convenient Conjunction, and that tiresome Interjection, the oddest of them all.

Now, as some of these Parts-of-Speech are richer, that is, have more words than others, and as they all like to have as many as they can get, it follows, I am sorry to say, that they are rather given to quarreling; and so it fell out that one day, when my story begins, they made so much noise, wrangling and jangling in the court, that they woke Judge Grammar up from a long and very comfortable nap.

"What is all this about?" he growled out, angrily. "Brother Parsing! Dr. Syntax! here!"

In an instant the Judge's two learned counselors were by his side.

Serjeant Parsing (Brother Parsing, the Judge calls him) has a sharp nose, bright eyes, a little round wig with a tail to it, and an eyeglass. He is very quick and cunning in finding out who people are and what they mean, and making them tell "the truth, the whole truth, and nothing but the truth." It is of no use to say "I don't know" to Serjeant Parsing. He will question you, and question you, till somehow or other he makes you know, and finds out all about you. When I say he will question *you*, of course I mean he will question the Parts-of-Speech, for that is his business, and that is why Judge Grammar summoned him. For whenever there is a fuss in Grammar Land, Serjeant Parsing has to find out all about it, and Dr. Syntax has to say what is right or wrong, according to the law.

"Brother Parsing," said the Judge, "this racket must be stopped. What are they fighting about? I divided the words clearly enough once amongst the nine Parts-of-Speech. Why cannot they keep the peace?"

"My lord," answered Serjeant Parsing, "the fact is that it is a long time since you portioned out the words, and the Parts-of-Speech since then have been left to do pretty much as they like. Some of them are greedy, and have stolen their neighbors' words. Some of them have got hold of new words, which the others say they had no right to make; and some of them are even inclined to think that Dr. Syntax is old fashioned, and need not be obeyed. In fact, unless your lordship takes the matter in hand at once, I am afraid the good old laws of Grammar Land will all go to wreck and ruin."

"That must never be," said the Judge, solemnly shaking his wig: "that must never be. We must stop it at once. Go and summon all my court before me."

"Certainly, my lord," answered Serjeant Parsing; "but may I ask if there is any Part-of-Speech you wish for in particular?"

"I wish for them all, sir, every one," replied the Judge. "They shall all come before me, and you shall question them in turn, and make them say what right they have to the titles and the words which they claim; and then if there is any disagreement between them, I will settle the matter once for all."

"Quite so, my lord," said Serjeant Parsing; "and shall I invite our friends in Schoolroom Shire?"

"Our friends in Schoolroom Shire? By all means let them come," replied the Judge. "If we wish to have peace among the Parts-of-Speech it is most important that the people of Matter-of-fact-land should know how to use them well. And as the people of Matter-of-fact-land generally spend at least a part of their lives in Schoolroom Shire, we cannot do better than send our invitation there. Go, Brother Parsing, and request them to come, and to bring their slates and pencils with them, that they may keep an account of what we do, and let our Parts-of-Speech prepare to come before us at once."

Away went Serjeant Parsing, as quick as thought, and soon the whole court was assembled, there was Judge Grammar on his throne, with a long flowing wig and gorgeous robes. At the table below him sat his two counselors, Serjeant Parsing and Dr. Syntax. Dr. Syntax is very tall and thin and dark. He has a long thin neck covered up with a stiff black tie, which looks as though it nearly choked him. When he speaks he stands up, looks straight through his spectacles, sticks out his chin, and says his say in a gruff and melancholy voice, as if he were repeating a lesson. He is the terror of all little boys, for he never smiles, and he is so very, very old, that people say he never was young like other folks; that when he was a baby he always cried in Greek, and that his first attempt at talking was in Latin. However that may be, there he sat, side by side with Serjeant Parsing, while the company from Schoolroom Shire, armed with slates and pencils, prepared to listen to the examination that was to take place, and the Parts-of-Speech crowded together at the end of the court, waiting for their names to be called.

Chapter 1
Mr. Noun

THE first Part-of-Speech that was called was Mr. Noun. He is a stout big fellow, very well dressed, for he does not mind showing that he is very rich.

As Mr. Noun came forward, Serjeant Parsing rose, put his pen behind his ear, arranged his papers on the table before him, and looking at Mr. Noun through his eyeglass, asked: "What is your name?"

"Name," answered Mr. Noun.

"Yes, your name?" repeated Serjeant Parsing.

"Name," again answered Mr. Noun.

"Do not trifle, sir," said the Judge, sternly; "what is your name? Answer at once, and truly."

"I have answered truly," replied Mr. Noun. "My name is *Name*, for *noun* means *name*. The name of everything belongs to me, so I am called Mr. Name, or Mr. Noun, which means the same thing, and all my words are called *nouns*."

"The name of *everything* belongs to you?" asked Serjeant Parsing, in surprise.

"Yes," answered Mr. Noun, "the name of everything."

"What? Do you mean to say that the name of everything I can see round me now is one of your words, and is called a noun?"

"I do indeed," said Mr. Noun. "The name of everything you can see, or touch, or taste, or smell, or hear, belongs to me."

"What," said Serjeant Parsing, "is this *desk* yours then, and the *ink* and the *pen* and the *window*?"

"The *words* that *name* them are all mine," said Mr. Noun. "Of course I have nothing to do with the *things*. No gentleman in Grammar Land has anything to do with *things*, only with words; and I assure you, you cannot *name* anything that you can see, or touch, or taste, or smell, or hear, without using one of my words. *Desk, pen, ink, window, water, wine, fire, smoke, light, lightning, thunder,* a *taste,* a *smell,* a *noise* all these words belong to me, and are called nouns."

"I see," said Serjeant Parsing; "you can *hear* thunder, and *smell* smoke, and *taste* wine. And I suppose *dinner* and *tea* are yours also?"

"Certainly, the *words* breakfast, dinner, and tea, are mine," replied Mr. Noun. "The *things* are what the people live upon in Schoolroom Shire, but they could not name what they eat without using my words. The servant would have to make signs to let people know that dinner was ready; she could not *say* so unless I allowed her to use my noun *dinner*.

"Well," said Serjeant Parsing, "if you have the name of everything we can see, touch, taste, smell, or hear, all I can say is, I hope you are satisfied, and do not claim any more words besides."

"Indeed," replied Mr. Noun, drawing himself proudly up, "I have not mentioned nearly all my words. I told you at first that I have the name of *everything*, and there are plenty of things that you know about, although you cannot see, or touch, or taste, or smell, or hear them. For instance, *love*, or *anger*, or *happiness*. You can feel them in your heart, and know they are there, although you cannot touch them with your fingers, or taste them with your tongue, or find them out by any of your five senses."

"Do you mean to say, then," asked Serjeant Parsing, "that when a child feels naughty in its heart—?"

"Naughtiness is mine," said Mr. Noun; "the *word* naughtiness, for it is the *name* of the something bad that the child feels."

"And when it is kind?"

"Kindness is mine, because it is the *name* of the something kind and nice it feels *there.* I have a good many more words that end in *ness,* and that are the names of things you can find out about, and talk about, though you cannot tell what shape or color or smell or taste they have; like *cleverness, silliness, idleness, ugliness, quickness.*"

"I see," said Serjeant Parsing. "You cannot tell what shape or color cleverness is, but you can soon find out whether a boy has any of it by the way in which he does his lessons."

"Yes," said Mr. Noun; "and the names of his lessons are mine too, for the lessons are things that you can learn about; *geography, history, writing, arithmetic,* all these names belong to me."

"Really Mr. Noun," said Serjeant Parsing, "you do claim a big share of words. You will be making out that the names of *persons* belong to you next."

"So they do," replied Mr. Noun; "no matter who the persons are, their names belong to me. I have the name of every person in the world from good Queen Victoria on her throne to the raggedest beggar-boy in the street. There is not a child in Schoolroom Shire whose name is not a noun. And I have not the names of *people* only, but of all pet dogs, cats, birds, horses, or rabbits: *Fido, Tabby, Bright-eye, Tiny, Shag,* and any other pet names you can think of. Indeed, I am very particular about such names. I call them *proper nouns,* and expect them always to be written with a capital letter."

"Proper nouns?" repeated Serjeant Parsing. "Then what are the other nouns called?"

"They are only *common* nouns," answered Mr. Noun, carelessly.

"Then all names are common nouns, except the names of persons or animals, are they?" asked Serjeant Parsing.

"No, no, no," said Mr. Noun, quite crossly: "the name of an animal is not a proper noun unless it is the own special name of one animal, that marks it from other animals of the same kind. *Dog* is the name given to all dogs, they have the name in common between them; but *Fido* is the name of one particular dog, his own proper name by which his master calls him. So *dog* is a common noun, *Fido* is a proper noun."

"Oh, I see," said Serjeant Parsing. "Then the particular name of any person or animal is a proper noun, and all other names are common nouns."

"I never said that," exclaimed Mr. Noun. "How very stup—I mean, you do not understand me, my dear sir. I never said that the particular name of a place or thing was not a proper noun too. Every particular and special name, whether of a person, an animal, a place, or a thing, is a proper noun. Every place has its own proper name, or should have. Every country and mountain and river and town in Europe is named with a *proper* noun. Why, you would not call *England* a common noun, I should hope? There are plenty of countries in the world, but there is only one country that is called by the proper name of dear old England. *Country* is a common noun, all countries have it in common, but when you want to speak of any particular country you use the proper nouns, *England, Scotland, Ireland, France, etc., etc.*"

"Well, I think we can understand that the particular names of *places* are proper nouns," said Serjeant Parsing; "but you spoke about *things* also. Surely things have no proper names? You do not give names to chairs and tables, and call them Mr. Leanback or Squire Mahogany?"

"Not exactly," answered Mr. Noun; "we do not name chairs and tables with proper names, but what do you say to houses? They are *things*, are they not? And you may have heard of such names as *Marlborough House, Springfield Cottage, Ivy Lodge.*"

"Well, no other things besides houses have proper names, have they?" said Serjeant Parsing.

"Books are things," said Mr. Noun, "and they all have proper names. So have ships and boats, *Warrior, Seafoam, Fairy,* or something of that sort. I have heard of a cannon which was called *Roarer*, and you ought to know that King Arthur's sword was named *Excalibur*. Indeed, you can give a proper name to anything you like that you want to distinguish from other things of the same sort."

"And all such proper names, or proper nouns, as you call them, must be written with a capital letter, must they? Whether they are the names of persons, animals, places, or things, little or big?"

"Sir," answered Mr. Noun, "littleness or bigness makes no difference. If you had a pet fly, and called it Silver-wing, Silver-wing must be written with a capital S, because it is a proper noun."

"Well, Mr. Noun," said Serjeant Parsing, "your ideas of what is *proper* seem to me rather peculiar, but I suppose Dr. Syntax has no objection, so I will say nothing."

Dr. Syntax silently bowed his head.

The Judge then spoke "Mr. Noun, you have claimed a great many words, and it remains to be seen whether all the other Parts-of-Speech agree to these words being yours. In order to find out whether they do or no, I will ask our friends from School-room Shire to write out, each of them, a list of twenty names, the names of anything they can *see, hear, touch, taste, smell,* or *think about*, or the *proper* names of any persons, animals, places, or things they know; and when next we meet I will read out what they have written, and we shall hear whether any one has any good reason to give why they should not be called nouns."

The Judge then rose from his seat, and every one left the court.

Chapter 2
Little Article

WHEN Judge Grammar next took his seat in court, a number of papers covered with words were handed up to him by Serjeant Parsing.

"They are the lists of names, my lord," he said, "which you asked the people of Schoolroom Shire to write for you,"

"Very good," said the Judge. "I will read some of the words aloud, and if any one thinks that they are not *nouns*, let him come forward and say so. And he began to read: *the garden, the house, the sky, a book, a bird, a fly,* when suddenly he was interrupted by a sound of bitter sobbing and crying.

"What is the matter?" he asked. "Who dares to interrupt the court?"

"It is this tiresome little Article, your lordship," said Serjeant Parsing, pushing forward a ragged little fellow, who was rubbing both fists into his eyes and crying bitterly. "He says he is being cheated, my lord; that he has only two words of his own in all Grammar Land, and that they are being used on these lists as if they belonged to Mr. Noun."

"Bring him up before me," said the Judge. "What is your name, sir?"

"My name is Article, or Little-joint," replied the little fellow. "I have only two words in all Grammar Land, *a* and *the*. I lend them to Mr. Noun whenever he asks for them fairly; but, your lordship, it is very hard," and here he began to cry again, "that they should be read as your lordship was reading them just now, as if they belonged to Mr. Noun, when he is so rich, and I am so very, very poor."

"Is it true, Brother Parsing," asked the Judge, "that little Article is always ready to wait upon Mr. Noun?"

"Quite true, my lord," answered Serjeant Parsing.

"Indeed, I have often been able to discover Mr. Noun by catching sight of little Article running before him, for whenever you see an *a* or a *the*, you may be sure that Mr. Noun will have a word of his own in somewhere near. The chief use of little Article is to point out that a noun is coming, for you may be sure that if you can put an *a* or a *the* before a word, that word is a noun, as *a bird, the sky*."

And do you use him as much before your pet proper nouns, sir?" asked Judge Grammar of Mr. Noun.

"No, your lordship," replied Mr. Noun, "that I do not. Indeed, I cannot see that little Article is of much use to me at any time; but he has an old habit of coming with me wherever I go, and when I have no one else I do not mind having him."

"Well," said Judge Grammar, "if you do have him, take care that you use him well; and pray, Brother Parsing, tell the Schoolroom Shire children to give him a separate mark for himself, and not to put his words with Mr. Noun's."

"Certainly, my lord," said Serjeant Parsing, "but I have one question to ask first. This little Article said that he had only two words in all Grammar Land, *a* and *the*. I wish to ask him what he says to *an*, as you say *an* egg, *an* apple? Surely *an* belongs to him also."

Article was just beginning to answer when he suddenly stopped, turned pale, trembled, and looked as if he would have tumbled to pieces in terror, for he saw Dr. Syntax rise.

Dr. Syntax stood upright, looking very tall and thin and black: he spoke in very stern voice, but all he said was, "*An* is only used before a vowel or an *h* mute." Then he sat down again.

"Ah!" said Serjeant Parsing, drawing a long breath, "thank you. Now, little Article, say what you have to say."

"I have only to say," remarked Article, recovering his courage, "that *a* and *an* are really one and the same word; *a* is only *an* with his coat off. I like to use it best as *a* without its coat, but before a vowel or an *h* mute I am obliged," and here Article gave a frightened look at Dr. Syntax, "I am obliged to keep its coat on and call it *an*."

"And do you know what you mean by a vowel or an *h* mute?" asked Judge Grammar.

"O yes, my lord: there are five vowels, *a, e, i, o, u,*" answered Article.

"And what is an *h*-mute?" asked the Judge.

"An *h* that is not sounded, as in *an hour, an honor,*" answered Article, rather impatiently, for he was getting very tired of being questioned.

"And you are to use *an* before any word that begins with a vowel, *a, e, i, o,* or *u,* or an *h*-mute, are you?" asked the Judge.

"Yes, my lord," said Article, "I told you so before."

"Give us some examples of words beginning with each of these," said the Judge, "and show us how you use *an* before them."

Article held up one hand, with the thumb and four fingers stretched out, and pointing to each one in turn, beginning with the thumb, he answered: "*An* apple, *an* eagle, *an* idol, *an* ox, and *an* ugly, uncomfortable, unkind old Judge, to keep me here so long answering questions." Saying which, little ragged Article turned and scampered off as fast as his legs could carry him.

Serjeant Parsing then said that as Article had behaved so badly, he hoped the Judge would give him a severe punishment, by allowing the children of Schoolroom Shire to use his words as often as they liked in their new lists.

"Certainly," said Judge Grammar. "I request that each of you will write six new nouns, and will use an article before every one of them."

The court then rose, after Serjeant Parsing had handed the Schoolroom Shire children the following verse, begging them to find out all the nouns and articles in it:

> Once there was a little boy,
> With curly hair and pleasant eye;
> A boy who always spoke the truth,
> And never, never told a lie.

Chapter 3

Mr. Pronoun

WHEN the court next assembled, the Judge read aloud all the nouns and articles on the lists, casting a stern glance at little Article at each *a, an,* or *the* that he came to, in order to show that they were put in as a punishment for Article's impudent behavior the day before. Poor little Article said nothing, and no one having objected to any of the words, the Judge said: "Mr. Noun and Article, since no one finds fault with the words that you claim, I declare them to be lawfully yours. Now, stand aside, and let Mr. Pronoun come forward."

At these words Mr. Pronoun stood before the Judge. He is something like Mr. Noun, only he is thinner, and looks as if he worked harder.

"Mr. Pronoun?" said Serjeant Parsing, standing up to begin his questioning.

Mr. Pronoun bowed.

"Why are you called Pronoun, sir, and what words do you possess?"

"I am called Pronoun, because I often do the work for my rich neighbor, Mr. Noun. *Pro* means *instead of,* so *pronoun* means *instead of noun,* and my words are called *pro-*

nouns because they stand *instead of nouns*. Mr. Noun, though he is so rich, does not like to have his words used over and over again—he says it wears them out; so to save trouble I put in *my* little words, which do just as well."

"And you are not afraid of *your* words being worn out?" asked the Judge.

"O dear no! my lord," answered Pronoun. "I think my words are like the iron rails on the railway—the more they are used the brighter they look; it is only the idle ones that get rusty and spoilt. And it is not many of *my* words that get rusty, I can tell you, my lord. Serjeant Parsing knows how he was one day trying to make sense of Dr. Faustus without me, and what a muddle he made of it. If he will kindly repeat it now, I will show you."

So Serjeant Parsing said:

Dr. Faustus was a good man;
Dr. Faustus whipped Dr. Faustus's scholars now and then
When Dr. Faustus whipped the scholars Dr. Faustus made the scholars dance
Out of England into France

"There!" said Pronoun. "Let any one try to sing that, and he will find how awkward it is. Now, if you will use my little *he* or *his*, instead of saying Dr. Faustus so often, and put *them* instead of scholars, it will sound much better. Just listen. Please, Mr. Parsing, say it again, and I will come in when I am wanted."

So Serjeant Parsing said: "Dr. Faustus was a good man."

"*He* whipped *his*," shouted Pronoun.

"He whipped his scholars now and then. When—"

"*He* whipped *them*," shouted Pronoun.

"When he whipped them," continued Serjeant Parsing.

"*He* made *them* dance," cried Pronoun.

"When he whipped them he made them dance," repeated Serjeant Parsing, "out of England into France."

"Ah," said the Judge, "yes! It is certainly better so." Mr. Noun's words are not used so often, and all parties are pleased. Then *he, his,* and *them* are pronouns, as they stand instead of nouns. Now tell us what other words you have, Mr. Pronoun."

"First of all, my lord, I have words which are used instead of the names of people when they are talking of themselves, such as *I* or *me, we* or *us*. When a person is speaking of himself he does not name his own name, but says instead, *I* or *me*. Except, indeed, very little children, who say, 'Baby wants more,' or, 'Give baby milk.' Reasonable persons say, '*I* want more,' 'Give *me* some milk.'

"The Queen says *we* in speaking of herself," remarked the Judge.

"Yes, my lord," said Pronoun, "the Queen is of course allowed to use *we* or *us* when she means only herself; but other people do not use *we* or *us* unless they mean more than one person."

Then *I* or *me*, *we* or *us*, are the pronouns used instead of the names of people speaking of themselves, are they, Mr. Pronoun?" inquired Serjeant Parsing.

"Certainly," replied Pronoun: "and the words used instead of the names of persons you are *speaking to* are *thou*, or *thee*, and *you*. When I am speaking to you, Mr. Parsing, I say, I tell *you*; I do not say, I tell Serjeant Parsing."

"Quite so," answered Serjeant Parsing; "but why do you not say, I tell *thee*."

"Why, the fact is," replied Mr. Pronoun, "that *thou* and *thee* really stand for one person only, and *you* stands for more than one. But long ago people took it into their heads to fancy that it would be *very* polite to talk to one person as if he were at least as good as two. It is a very vulgar thing to be only one person, but to be two people rolled into one would be very grand indeed. So when a man was talking to a grand neighbor he called him *you* instead of *thou*, and the grand neighbor was so much pleased that it came to be the fashion to say *you* to every one, and my poor little *thou* and *thee* were quite set aside."

"And are they never used now?' said Serjeant Parsing. "O yes, they are used," said Mr. Pronoun; "but as people neglected them in former days, I won't have them used in common now. *You* is quite good enough for everyday talk."

"Well," said Serjeant Parsing, "you have shown that *I* or *me*, *we* or *us*, *thou* or *thee*, and *you*, are all your words. Have you any others?"

"Plenty more," answered Pronoun. "I have *he*, *she*, *it*, and *they*, to stand instead of persons or things you are talking about.

> Tom took Maria on the ice;
> *It* broke, and *she* fell in;
> *He* got a rope, and in a trice
> *He* pulled *her* out again.
> If *they* had both been drowned, you know,
> Folks would have said, "I told you so."

"There *it* stands for *ice*, and *she* for *Maria*, and *he* for *Tom*, and *they* for *Tom* and *Maria* together. So you see clearly that *he, she, it,* and *they* are pronouns."

"I do not think any one could deny it," said Serjeant Parsing. "Have you any other words?"

"O yes, there are plenty more words that stand instead of nouns. *My, thy, his, our, your, their,* which are used to show that something belongs to the person these words stand instead of. Just as instead of saying *Dr. Faustus's* scholars, we said *his* scholars; and as in speaking to you, my lord, I should not say Judge Grammar's wig, but *your* wig."

"You need not say anything about my wig," said the Judge, rather testily. "Mind your own words, sir, and tell us what others you have."

"I have *who* and *which,*" replied Pronoun. "Instead of saying, 'I met a man, the man had no eyes,' you say, 'I met a man *who* had no eyes; "so my little *who* saves Mr. Noun's man. Instead of saying, 'I will tell you a tale, a tale was told to me,' you can say, 'I will tell you a tale *which* was told to me;' so *which* stands instead of *tale.*"

"We understand," said the Judge. "No more of your tales now, if you please. You have no more words, I suppose?"

"Indeed I have, my lord. *This* and *that, these* and *those,* are pronouns. For when you say, 'Look at *this,*' you mean a picture, or a sum, or anything else that *this* may happen to stand for; and when you say, 'Take *that,*' *that* stands for a halfpenny, or a kick, or anything else you may be giving at the time. And if you sing to a child—if your lordship ever does sing—which does not seem very likely—"

"Mind your words, sir," said the Judge, again. "If we sing what?"

"If you sing '*This* is the way the lady goes,' then *this* stands for the jogging up and down of my knee, the way the lady goes."

"Really, Mr. Pronoun," said the Judge, "you are very childish. The Schoolroom Shire people are quite ashamed of you. We shall ask for no more of your words today, for I suppose, after all, they are easy enough to find out."

"All words that stand instead of nouns belong to me," said Pronoun; "but they are not quite so easy to find out as you suppose. Those that stand instead of persons, like *I, thou, he, we, you, they,* any one can find out. I have told you about a good many others, and if Serjeant Parsing wishes to discover the rest for himself—"

"He does, sir," said the Judge, who was getting very tired and hungry. "You may go. I will only ask you to assist our Schoolroom Shire friends in making the following verses right. They read very queerly at present; but if you can set them right, I think we shall agree that what you have been saying of your words is true."

The Judge then wished them all good morning, and went to lunch off a few pages of dictionary.

Here are the verses:

> There was a man, the man had no eyes,
> And the man went out to view the skies;
> The man saw a tree with apples on,
> The man took no apples off, and left no apples on.
>
> Little Bo-peep has lost Bo-peep's sheep,
> And does not know where to find the sheep;
> Leave the sheep alone till the sheep come home,
> And bring the sheep's tails behind the sheep.
>
> Matilda dashed the spectacles away
> To wipe Matilda's tingling eyes;
> And as in twenty bits the spectacles lay,
> Matilda's grandmamma Matilda spies.

Chapter 4
Serjeant Parsing's Visit

SERJEANT PARSING paid a visit to Schoolroom Shire.

"My young friends," he said, in his most amiable voice, "may I trouble you with a little piece of business for Judge Grammar today. I have here a story, and the Judge requests that you will kindly find out how many of the words in it belong to Mr. Noun, how many to Mr. Pronoun, and how often little ragged Article comes in. The best way to do this is to get your slates, and mark off a piece for Mr. Noun, another for Mr. Pronoun, and a corner somewhere for little Article. Write their names in each. Now I will read the story, and whenever I come to a noun, give Mr. Noun a mark; whenever I read a pronoun, give a mark to Mr. Pronoun; and if I read an *a*, *an*, or *the*, put down a mark to little Article. When it is finished we will count up and see who has the most marks."

Serjeant Parsing then read the following story:

"Some sailors belonging to a ship of war had a monkey on board. The monkey had often watched the men firing off a cannon, so one day when they were all at

dinner he thought he should like to fire it too. So he took a match, as he had seen the men do, struck it, put it to the touch hole, and looked into the mouth of the cannon, to see the ball come out. The ball did come out, and alas! alas! the poor little monkey fell down dead."

Chapter 5
Mr. Adjective

THE next Part-of-Speech called up before Judge Grammar was Mr. Adjective.

"My young friends in Schoolroom Shire," said Serjeant Parsing, "must know Mr. Adjective well. He is the greatest chatterbox and the veriest gossip that ever lived. You never in all your life, my lord, knew any one who could say so much about one thing as Mr. Adjective. Mr. Noun cannot mention a word, but Mr. Adjective is ready to tell all about it, whether it is *little* or *big*, *blue* or *green*, *good* or *bad*, and mischief enough he does in Schoolroom Shire. For instance, Mr. Noun mentions Willy's pen—'*Nasty, spluttering, cross-nibbed* thing,' whispers Adjective, and Willy thinks that is why he wrote such a bad copy, and did not dot his *i*'s. If Mr. Noun points out pussy, who is coming into the room, purring and rubbing her head against the leg of each chair as she passes, Adjective whispers that she is a '*dear, sweet, soft, warm, little* pet,' so Milly leaves off her sums to pick her up and play with her. Ann, the housemaid, finds dirty boot marks on her nice clean stairs, and as soon as she sees Tom she tells him he is a '*tiresome, untidy, disobedient,* and *naughty* boy,' not knowing that Mr. Adjective was whispering all those words in her ear. Indeed, Mr. Adjective causes more quarrels in Schoolroom Shire, and other places too, than any one can tell. Only yesterday Jane and Lucy had a quarrel, I hear, because Jane pulled the arm off Lucy's doll. If Adjective had not put into Lucy's head to call Jane *naughty* and *unkind*, Jane would not have answered that Lucy was *cross* and *disagreeable*. She would most likely have said, 'I beg your pardon, I did not mean to do it,' and they would have been friends again directly. See how much mischief is caused by talkative, gossiping Mr. Adjective."

"Really, Mr. Parsing," remarked Adjective, now putting in his word for the first time, "you have made a long speech to show how mischievous I am. Pray, have you nothing to say about the good that my kind, loving words do?"

"Oh, certainly, my dear sir," said Serjeant Parsing, suddenly changing his tone. "When you like any one you are a very good-natured fellow, and can say all sorts of sweet things, I heard you in Schoolroom Shire telling Mary that her mamma is her *own dearest, kindest, sweetest* mother—that baby is a *bright, bonny little* darling—that Fido is a *good, faithful old* doggie—and that home is the *happiest* place in the *whole wide* world. Oh, yes," continued Serjeant Parsing, "you can call people good names as well as bad."

"I do not call people names," said Adjective, indignantly. "I *qualify* them. I could qualify you, Mr. Parsing, and say you are an *impertinent, rude*—"

"That will do, Mr. Adjective," interrupted the Judge. "We understand what you mean by *qualifying*. But tell us, are your words always placed *before* nouns?"

"Oh, no, my lord," answered Adjective. "They *can*, almost all of them, be used before a noun, but they are often used after it, in this way:

The sky is *blue*,
The sun is *bright*,
My words are *true*,
The snow is *white*.

"You could also say, *blue sky, bright sun, true words, white snow*, but it does not sound so well, I think. And when a pronoun stands instead of a noun, and my words qualify it—"

"Oh, you qualify pronouns as well as nouns, do you?" asked Serjeant Parsing.

"I am obliged to do so sometimes," said Mr. Adjective, rather sulkily. "I will not have my words used before a pronoun, as they are before a noun. You can say:

I am *right*,
And *you* are *wrong*:

It is *late,*
And *we* are *strong.*

But you must not say: *right I, wrong you, late it,* or *strong we.*"

"I should think not," said Serjeant Parsing, laughing. "Then we are to understand that adjectives are used to qualify nouns and pronouns, and that they may be used before a noun or after it, but not before a pronoun."

"Quite right, so far," said Mr. Adjective; "but I can do other things besides qualifying nouns."

"What can you do?"

"I can tell how many there are of the thing the noun names, *one, two, three, four,* and so on. And whether the thing is the *first, second, third,* or *fourth,* and so on. And whether there are *some* things, *many* things, *few* things, *more* things, *no* things."

"And all these words are adjectives, are they?"

"Yes," answered Adjective. "All words that can be put before *thing* or *things* are adjectives."

"*A* thing, *the* thing," remarked little Article, looking up with a cunning smile at Adjective. "*A* and *the* are both articles."

"*A* and *the* don't count, of course," said Adjective, impatiently. "Besides, they were adjectives once, people say, only they got so worn out, that I let my ragged little cousin Article have them. But except *a* and *the,* there is no word that you can put before *thing* or *things* that is not an adjective. *A beautiful thing,* an *ugly thing, bad things, good things, green things, yellow things, large things, little things;* and so you can say, *one thing, two things, some things, any things;* and also, *this thing, that thing, these things, those things.*"

"That seems a very easy way of finding out an adjective," remarked the Judge. "I hope it is a correct way."

"Indeed it is, my lord," said Adjective, earnestly. "See, I can give you many more examples.

A *lovely, graceful, beautiful* thing,
A *useful, homely, dutiful* thing;
Foolish, childish, useless things;
Handsome, rich, and *priceless* things."

"My lord," said Mr. Noun, coming forward and speaking in a solemn voice, "I accuse Mr. Adjective of stealing, and wish him to be sent to prison."

"Indeed!" said the Judge; "but he must be tried first, I and you must prove him guilty before I have him punished. What do you say he has stolen?"

"My lord, he is constantly stealing my words, and only just now he used these without my leave, in open court: *love, grace, beauty, use, home, duty.*"

"Enough," said the Judge. "I certainly heard him use some such words only just now. Critics," he called to the policemen, for that is the name they have in Grammar Land, "seize Mr. Adjective, and keep him safe until the court meets again, when he shall be tried for stealing." Then turning to the people of Schoolroom Shire, the Judge continued, "My friends, I shall be much obliged if you will look over the following story, and strike out of it all the words belonging to Mr. Adjective. I cannot allow them to remain side by side with other words, until it is proved that Mr. Adjective is not guilty of stealing them."

The Judge then rose, and poor Mr. Adjective was led out of the court, with his hands bound.

The following is the story which the Judge sent to the people of Schoolroom Shire.

THE MAIDEN PRINCE

A long, long time ago, there lived in a grey old castle, a widowed queen, who had one only child, a beautiful bright boy. "My good husband was killed in the terrible war," said the timid queen, "and if my dear son grows up to be a strong man, I fear that he will go to the cruel wars, too, and be killed. So he shall learn nothing about rough war, but shall be brought up like a simple maiden." So she taught him all maidenly duties, to spin, and to weave, and to sew, and she thought he was too simple and quiet to wish to go to war; but one day there came to the great castle gate a noble knight riding a gallant charger. "Come," he cried to the young prince, "come, follow me. I ride to fight with the wicked and strong who are oppressing the weak and the poor." Up sprang, in a moment, the fair young boy, flung aside his girlish work, seized his father's battered sword, and leaped into the saddle behind the noble knight. "Farewell, dear mother," he cried, "no more girlish work for me. I must be a brave man, as my father was, and conquer or die in the rightful cause." Then the foolish queen saw that it was useless to try to make a daring boy into a timid maiden.

Chapter 6

Mr. Adjective Tried for Stealing

THERE was great excitement in the court the next day; and when every one was assembled, except Adjective, the Judge called out: "Bring the prisoner in;" and poor Adjective was led in between two Critics, with his hands tied behind him, and placed before the Judge.

Serjeant Parsing rose, and began to question him.

"Is your name Adjective?" he said. "It is," answered Adjective.

"And you possess all the adjectives in Grammar Land?"

"I do."

"What is an adjective?"

"A word used to qualify a noun."

"What is a noun?"

"Please, my lord, need I answer that?" asked Adjective.

"Certainly," replied the Judge.

"It is not fair," said Adjective; "nouns are not my words."

"But you must know what a noun is, in order that you must use your adjectives properly."

Of course I know what a noun is—it is a *name*, the name of anything."

"Then do you know the difference between a noun and an adjective?" asked Serjeant Parsing.

"Certainly. A *noun* is the name of a thing. An *adjective* tells you something about the thing the noun has named; whether it is large or small, or what color it is, or how much there is of it, or whether there are few things or many, or something of that sort."

"Quite so; but can you find out at once, without much thinking, whether a word is a noun or an adjective?"

"If you can put an article before a word, then it is a noun," answered Adjective; "as, *a* man, *the* dog."

"Then when I say, 'Pity the poor,' of course *poor* is a noun, is it?"

"No," said Adjective, quickly; "*poor* is my word, I know, for you can say *poor* child, a *poor* thing. 'Pity the poor' really means, 'Pity the poor people;' but Mr. Noun is so stingy, that when he thinks the sentence will be understood without his word, he just leaves it out, and then people say the noun is *understood*."

"Exactly so; but your way of finding out a noun does not answer, you see, for the first time I try it, you tell me the word I have found is an adjective."

It always answers unless there happens to be a word understood," replied Adjective, "and then it answers if you use your reason; for any one would know that you are not asked to pity a thing called a *poor*, but to pity poor people. But it is not fair, my lord," continued Adjective, turning to the Judge. "Here am I, a poor prisoner, unjustly accused of stealing, and Mr. Parsing is trying to puzzle me as much as he can."

"Not at all," replied Serjeant Parsing. "I only want you to be sure that you know clearly the difference between a noun and an adjective."

"I do," answered Adjective, "quite clearly."

"Well, then, answer this question. What is the word *beauty*?

"Beauty?" repeated Adjective, getting rather red; *beauty* is a noun."

"Yes," said Serjeant Parsing; "and *grace*, and *home*, and *duty*?"

"They are all nouns," answered Adjective, looking uncomfortable.

"Yes; now another question. What is *beautiful*?"

"Beautiful?" repeated Adjective, looking *very* red now; "*beautiful* is an adjective."

"Very well. Now, Mr. Adjective," said Serjeant Parsing, "kindly tell me how you got the adjective *beautiful*?"

"I made it," answered Adjective, with his eyes on the ground.

"How did you make it?"

I stuck *ful* on to *beauty*; When I want to say a thing is full of beauty I call it *beautiful*."

And how did you get *beauty*, since it belongs to Mr. Noun?" asked Serjeant Parsing.

"I took it," replied Adjective, still looking down.

"Which means to say that you stole it. It is quite clear that you stole it, and that you did the same to *grace, home, duty*, and others, to make *graceful, homely, dutiful*, and the rest. My lord, I think I need say nothing more: the prisoner himself owns that he took these words; it only remains for you to give him his punishment."

The Judge looked very grave, and was beginning to say, "Mr. Adjective, I am very sorry—" when Serjeant Parsing interrupted him, and said:

"Please, my lord, I am going to take the other side now. Will you order Mr. Noun to come forward to be questioned?"

"Certainly," said the Judge; and Mr. Noun approached.

"Mr. Noun?" said Serjeant Parsing.

"The same, sir," said Mr. Noun; "all nouns belong to me."

"You know a noun when you see it?"

"Of course I know my own words."

"And you know an adjective?"

"Yes; an adjective is a word that tells something about one of my nouns."

"Very good. Now can you tell me whether *happy* is a noun?"

"Certainly not. It is an adjective. You can say a happy boy, a happy thing."

"Exactly so. Now will you tell me what *happiness* is?"

"Happiness," repeated Mr. Noun, getting suddenly very red, for he saw what was coming; "happiness is a noun, it is mine."

"Oh!" said Serjeant Parsing; "how did you get it?"

"I made it."

"How?"

"I joined *happy* and *ness* together."

"H'm!" said Serjeant Parsing. "I will not ask you where you found such a silly word as *ness*, but *happy* you said just now belongs to Mr. Adjective, so of course you took it from him."

 Mr. Noun did not answer, but looked down, exceedingly red and uncomfortable.

"My lord," said Serjeant Parsing to the Judge, "need I say any more. This Mr. Noun, who would have Adjective put in prison for stealing, has been doing the very same thing himself. *Happiness, prettiness, silliness, cleverness,* and almost all the words that end in *ness,* are nouns made from adjectives. If Mr. Noun would give them all up, I have no doubt Mr. Adjective would then give up his *beautiful, useful, graceful,* and other adjectives that are made from nouns."

"No, no," said the Judge; "I will have no giving up. When a word is once made it is made for good, and instead of blaming those who take their neighbor's words to make new ones for themselves, I consider that they are very much to be praised. Critics, untie Mr. Adjective's hands. Mr. Adjective, I am glad to hear you are so clever in making new words, and I give you full permission to make as many more as you can, by borrowing either from Mr. Noun or from any other Part-of-Speech. Have you any other ending to put on besides *ful*?"

"My lord," said Adjective, whose hands were now untied, and who was standing free and upright before the Judge, "my lord, I have a whole string of tails which I keep ready to make adjectives with. Here are some of them: *ful, like, ly, y, ous, less, en,* and *ern*; and this is the way I stick them on: *beautiful, ladylike, manly, dirty, poisonous, careless, golden, western,* and with your lordship's kind permission, I will make such words as often as I can."

"Do so," replied the Judge. "And you, Mr. Noun, remember, that you are to allow Adjective to take your words whenever he requires them, for you ought to know that words in Grammar Land are not like pennies in Matter-of-fact-land. *There,* if some one steals a penny from you, he has it and you have not; but *here,* in Grammar Land, when any one takes your words to make new ones, it makes him richer, but you are none the poorer for it. You have *beauty* still, although Mr. Adjective has made *beautiful*; and you have *lady,* and *man,* and *gold,* although Mr. Adjective has made *ladylike,* and *manly,* and *golden.* You ought to have known this, Mr. Noun, and not to have accused Mr. Adjective of stealing. Therefore, as a punishment, I require you to send into Schoolroom

Shire a list of nouns that may be made into adjectives by the addition of some of Mr. Adjective's tails."

The Judge then left the court, and this is the list that Mr. Noun sent into School-room Shire.

Nouns to be made into Adjectives.

Truth	Lady	Child	Dirt
Faith	Man	Baby	Wood
Hope	Love	Fool	Fire
Care	Gold	North	Poison
Sleep	Wood	East	Danger
Sense	Silk	West	Virtue

Adjective endings that may be added to Nouns.

-ful	-like or -ly	-ish	-y
-less	-en	-ern	-ous (meaning full of)

Chapter 7
The Quarrel Between Mr. Adjective &
Mr. Pronoun & Little Interjection

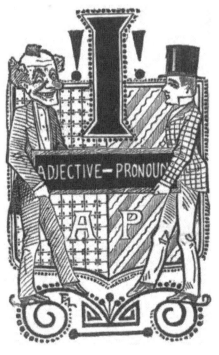

IT is sad to tell that nearly the first thing Mr. Adjective did when he was set free was to have a quarrel with Pronoun.

When the Judge came into court the next day he found them both much excited.

"It is mine, I know it is," said Pronoun.

"And I know it is mine," cried Adjective. "I'll ask the Judge if it is not."

"I'll ask him, too," said Pronoun. "My lord," he continued, coming forward, "*her* is mine, and Adjective wants to take it from me. But when I claimed it in court before, he said nothing about it."

"I thought the more," returned Adjective, "but I supposed that you would give it up quietly without all this fuss in court."

"I would willingly give it up if it were yours," said Pronoun; "but it is not."

"It is," cried Adjective, angrily; "I tell you it is.

"Silence!" said the Judge, sternly. "Brother Parsing, be kind enough to question both Adjective and Pronoun, that we may know the cause of this quarrel, and hear what each has to say for himself."

"Certainly, my lord," answered Serjeant Parsing. "Adjective, what words do you claim?"

"*My, thy, his, her, its, our, your,* and *their,*" replied Adjective.

"Well, Mr. Pronoun, tell us how you make them out to be yours."

"Nothing is easier," answered Pronoun. "These words stand instead of nouns, and therefore they must be pronouns. When you say '*my thumb,*' my lord, you mean Judge Grammar's thumb, so *my* stands instead of the noun Judge Grammar. And when you say, 'Little Bo-peep has lost *her* sheep,' you mean *Little Bo-peep's* sheep, therefore *her* stands instead of *Little Bo-peep.* So *my* and *her* are clearly pronouns; and *thy, his, its, your, their,* are used in just the same way, and therefore must be pronouns too."

"It would seem so," said the Judge. "What has Mr. Adjective to say to that?"

"I will soon tell you, my lord," replied Adjective. "You will, of course, allow that an adjective is a word that may be used before a noun, to tell something about the thing that the noun names. It has been said that if you can put thing or things after a word, that word (not counting *a* or *the,* of course) is sure to be an adjective; as, a *good thing,* a *bad thing, large things, little things,* and so on. Well, I am sure you can say *my* thing, *thy* thing, *his* thing, *her* thing, *its* thing, *our* thing, *your* thing, and *their* thing. Therefore, *my, thy, his, her, its, our, your,* and *their,* must be adjectives."

"H'm! It is all very well to say *must,*" remarked the Judge, "but then Pronoun says they *must* be pronouns. Are there any more of your words, Mr. Pronoun, that Adjective claims in the same way?"

"My lord," answered Pronoun, "he claims all the words of mine that may be used before a noun. *This, that, these,* and *those,* for instance."

"Of course I do," said Adjective; "for when you say *this* bird, *that* horse, *these* rabbits, *those* people; *this, that, these,* and *those* are clearly used with a noun, but do not stand instead of one."

"Ah!" said Pronoun, "but when you say 'look at *this,*' 'take *that,*' 'may I have *these?*' 'burn *those;*' this, that, these, and those are *not* used it *with* a noun, but clearly stand *instead of* one, and therefore they are pronouns."

"It seems to me," said the Judge, half to himself, "that sometimes they are adjectives, and sometimes they are pronouns,"

"That is just what I say, my lord," cried Adjective, "and if you will allow it, I think I know of a way that will make peace between us directly. Let us call them *Adjec-*

tive-pronouns, and have them between us. When they are used, not with a noun, but instead of one, then Pronoun may have them all to himself; but when they are used like adjectives, before a noun, then we will have them between us, and call them *adjective-pronouns*."

"That seems very fair," replied the Judge, "and I certainly allow it. Mr. Pronoun, be kind enough to give us a list of your words, and Mr. Adjective will point out any that may be used as adjective-pronouns."

So Mr. Pronoun began: "*I, thou, he, she, it, we, you, they, mine, thine, his, hers, its, ours, yours, theirs; my, thy, his, her, its, our, your, their.*"

"Those last eight are between us," said Adjective, "for they can all be used before a noun."

"*Myself, thyself, himself, herself, itself, ourselves, yourselves, or yourself, themselves,*" said Pronoun, with a little toss of his head, "those, at least, are all mine, Mr. Adjective."

"Continue repeating your words, sir," said the Judge, sternly; "do not stop to talk."

"*This, that, these, those,*" continued Pronoun.

"Adjective-pronouns, all four of them," remarked Mr. Adjective; "we have shown that already."

"*Each, either, neither, one, other,*" continued Pronoun.

"Stop," said the Judge; "we have not had these words before. You must give us some sentences to show that they are pronouns."

Pronoun replied:

> Two sparrows had a fight today,
> *Each* wished to take a worm away;
> *One* pulled at it, so did the *other*,
> *Neither* would yield it to his brother,
> Had *either* given up at least,
> His brother would have had the feast;
> But while they fought a thrush came by,
> And with the worm away did fly.

"There, my lord," continued Pronoun, "all the words, *each, one, other, neither, either,* stand for sparrow in those lines, and as sparrow is a noun, they must be pronouns."

"They are adjective-pronouns sometimes," remarked Mr. Adjective, "for you can say, *each* boy,' 'the *other* day,' 'on *either* side.' "

"Certainly," said the Judge. "Have you any more, Mr. Pronoun?"

"*Who, which, what,*" continued Pronoun.

"You must show that they are pronouns," said the Judge.

"Here is the man *who* shot the tiger," said Pronoun.

" 'Here are two apples; *which* do you choose?' 'I know *what* I want.' *Who* stands instead of the *man*, because you could say, 'Here is the man; the man shot the tiger.' *Which* stands instead of one of the apples, and *what* stands instead of the thing that I want, whatever it may be."

"Yes," said Serjeant Parsing. "But if *who* and *what* are used to ask questions, as, '*who* is there?' '*what* is that?' then what do *who* and *what* stand instead of?"

If you will answer the questions, and tell me who was really there, and what that really was, then I will tell you what nouns *who* and *what* stand instead of; but if you do not know any answer to your own questions, then of course I cannot tell you what noun my little pronouns stand for; I can only tell you they stand instead of something, and therefore are pronouns."

"*Which* and *what* are used before nouns sometimes," cried Adjective: " '*which* way are you going?' '*what* bell is that?' therefore they are adjective-pronouns too."

At any rate," said Pronoun, haughtily, "*who* is altogether mine, for you cannot say, 'who way,' 'who book,' 'who man,' or anything of that sort."

"Hoo! hoo! hoo! ha! ha! ha! he! he! he!" cried a voice among the crowd "Old Adjective beaten! hurrah! bravo!"

Every one in the court looked round to see where such strange sounds came from.

"It is Interjection," said Serjeant Parsing, angrily, making a dive at the crowd behind him, to try and catch hold of some one in it."

"Critics," cried the Judge," seize that fellow, and bring him here."

But that was more easily said than done, for little Interjection was as quick and active as any street boy in London. He dodged in and out amongst the other Parts-of-Speech, and was here, there, and everywhere, till at last he tumbled up against Serjeant Parsing, who held him fast till the Critics came up. He is such an odd little creature, that you could hardly tell what he is like. One moment he is crying bitterly, and the next he is in fits of laughter; when you look at him again he is perhaps shrieking for fear, and in another minute he is standing on his head for joy. He is so fond of standing on his head, that people say he had his portrait taken so once (!), and that is why they put a note of exclamation (!) after his words; but that is all nonsense, of course.

"Interjection!" said the Judge, sternly, "you are the last of all the Parts-of-Speech, and have no business to interrupt the court now. Let me not hear you again until your turn comes."

"Alas! alas!" cried Interjection, wringing his hands. "Mr. Parsing says I am only a poor little fellow thrown in (that is what my name interjection means, *thrown in*), to express surprise or fear, joy or sorrow. When folks do not know what to say next, one of my little words pops in, and poor Mr. Parsing is at his wit's end to know what to do with it, ah! ah! Off! off!" he cried, changing his tone, and suddenly jerking himself out of the policeman's hold. "Away! away!" he shouted, springing to the door; and before they could catch him he was indeed away, and they heard his "ha! ha! ha!" die away in the distance.

Serjeant Parsing then turned to the Schoolroom Shire folks, and asked them to mark off on their slates places for Mr. Noun, Pronoun, Adjective, and little Article, and a corner somewhere for tiresome Interjection; and while he read to them, to put down a stroke in the right place for each word that they knew. "And when you come to an adjective-pronoun used *with* a noun," continued Serjeant Parsing, "put a stroke on the line that divides Adjective's ground from Pronoun's. That will be like a little man sitting astride on the wall, with one leg for Pronoun to pull and one for Adjective. Of course if it is used *instead* of a noun, and *not* with one, then Mr. Pronoun must have the stroke all to himself. Whichever Part-of-Speech gets the most strokes gains the game."

This is what Serjeant Parsing read.

"Alas! alas! that naughty boy," said Harry's mother, as she waited for him to come back from school. "He must have gone to play with the other boys at the big pond, and he will certainly fall in, for the boys are sure to try the ice, and it is too thin to bear them yet. Oh! my poor, dear boy! what shall I do? If he falls into the black, cold water, he will certainly be drowned. My darling Harry! ah! why does he not come home? If I had any one to send...Why, there he is, I declare, with his hands full of oranges. Oh! the naughty boy! I will give him a great scolding. To give me a fright, and keep me waiting while he was buying oranges! Harry, you are a naughty, careless, tiresome —What! kissing me, you little rogue, to stop my mouth. There! there! do not pull down my hair, and never give your poor mother such a fright again; and now come in and see the lovely Christmas box I have for you."

Chapter 8
Dr. Verb

THE next Part-of-Speech called up before Judge Grammar, to give an account of himself, was Dr. Verb.

He came bustling up with an air of great importance.

"My lord, my name is Verb. I am called Verb because *verb* means *word*, and the verb is the most important word, *the* word, in fact, in every sentence."

"The *most important* word!" cried Mr. Noun, interrupting him. "My lord, he says the verb is the most important word in every sentence! Why, Dr. Verb, you know that *you* cannot give the name of a single thing, for all names are nouns, and belong to me. The *verb* the most important word, indeed, when I have the name of everything!"

"I know that," answered Dr. Verb, "I know very well that when people want to name a thing they must use a noun. But do you suppose that when they have simply named a thing they have made a sentence? Not a bit of it. To make a sentence you must tell something about the thing that you have named; you must say whether it *is* or *has* or *does* anything, as: 'Ice *is* cold,' 'Puss *has* a tail,' 'Blackbirds *sing*.' *Is*, *has*, *sing*, are verbs, and so are all words that speak of *being*, *having*, or *doing*, and without some such word you cannot make a sentence."

"You think so, Dr. Verb," said the Judge, "but I should like it to be proved. Brother Parsing, just call some of the other Parts-of-Speech forward, and let them try to make a sentence without Dr. Verb."

"I will, my lord," answered Serjeant Parsing. "Noun, Adjective, and Article, be kind enough to step forward, and each of you give me a word."

"*Sun*," said Mr. Noun.

"*Bright*," said Adjective.

"*The*," said little Article.

"Very good," said Serjeant Parsing, "now I will put them together; '*sun bright the;*' '*the bright sun;*' '*the sun bright.*' They do not seem to make quite a proper sentence, my lord, any way."

"Of course not," said Dr. Verb, interrupting; "for when you say '*the bright sun,*" which sounds the best of the three ways, you still have not made a sentence, for you have not said whether the bright sun is shining, or is not shining, or whether you can see it, or what it does. '*The sun bright*' of course is nonsense; but say the sun *is* bright, and then you tell a fact about the sun, and you have made a sentence fit to set before the king."

"You had better try Mr. Noun again, Brother Parsing," said Judge Grammar. "Perhaps he can give you a more convenient word."

Serjeant Parsing turned again to Mr. Noun, and asked for another word.

"'*Hippopotamus*," answered Mr. Noun. Mr. Adjective gave *fat*.

"Now, little Article, give me *a*," said Serjeant Parsing, "and I will put them together. '*Hippopotamus fat a;*' '*a fat hippopotamus;*' '*a hippopotamus fat.*' H'm! it sounds odd."

"'*A fat hippopotamus*' does not sound wrong," put in Mr. Noun.

"Not wrong, of course," answered Dr. Verb. "You may mention a fat hippopotamus, if you like, or any other animal, but unless you tell something about it you have not made a sentence. Say that it *is*, or *has*, or *did* something, if you want to make a sentence; like 'a fat hippopotamus is here;' or 'a hippopotamus has a fat body;' or, 'a hippopotamus ate me up,' or, 'swam away,' or something of that sort. Then you will have some famous sentences, but you will have had to use verbs to make them, for *is, has, ate, swam*, are all verbs, for they are all words that speak of *being, having*, or *doing*."

"How can we always find out if a word is a verb?" asked Serjeant Parsing.

"It is sure to be a verb if you can put a little *to* before it," answered Dr. Verb; "*to be, to have, to do, to eat, to drink, to swim, to fly, to speak, to think, to run, to dance, to play, to sing, to sleep, to wake, to laugh, to cry, to call, to fall;*" and Dr. Verb stopped, quite out of breath.

"That sounds very easy," said Serjeant Parsing. "Let me try it with the words that you said were verbs; *to is, to has, to ate, to swam.*"

"Stop, stop," cried Dr. Verb; "not like that. You must not put *to* before any part of the verb you like. *Is* is part of the verb *to be, has* is part of the verb *to have.*"

"*Is*, part of the verb *to be*!" said Serjeant Parsing. "What do you mean? Why, the two words have not a single letter alike."

"True; but still they mean the same sort of thing. When a countryman says 'he *be* a brave lad,' he means the same thing as 'he *is* a brave lad;' or when he says, 'I *be* too tired,' he means, "I *am* too tired.' *Is* and *am* ought to be used according to the laws of Grammar Land instead of *be*, but as they both express something about *being* they are said to be parts of the verb *to be*. In the same way *has* is part of the verb *to have, ate* is part of the verb *to eat*, and *swam* is part of the verb *to swim*.

"That is very learned, I daresay," said Serjeant Parsing, "but will you kindly tell us, Dr. Verb, how we are to guess that *am*, or any other word that has neither a *b* nor an *e* in it, is part of the verb *to be*?"

"You cannot *guess*, of course," retorted Dr. Verb, sharply. "I never said you were to guess. You must use your reason, to find out whether they have the same sort of meaning. Or if you like it better, learn the song that Mr. Pronoun and I have made up, to bring in all the different parts of the verb."

"A song?" said Judge Grammar, in surprise. "I did not know that you could sing, Dr. Verb; but let us hear your song, by all means."

"If you will not interrupt me, my lord, I will give you three verses of it," answered Dr. Verb.

"No, we will not interrupt," said the Judge.

So Dr. Verb began:

The Song of the Verb "To Be"

Present Tense

I am	We are
Thou art	You are
He is	They are

Past Tense

I was	We were
Thou wast	You were
He was	They were

Future Tense

I shall be	We shall be
Thou wilt be	You will be
He will be	They will be

When he had finished, everyone burst out laughing.

"And you call that singing, do you, Dr. Verb?" said the Judge.

"Dr. Syntax, there, calls it *conjugating*, I believe," said Dr. Verb; "but I think *singing* is a prettier and easier name for it,"

"But it is not a song at all," said the Judge, nearly laughing again; "there is no tune in it, and no rhyme."

"It is the best that Pronoun and I could make alone," said Dr. Verb, angrily. "But it can be easily made to rhyme if the other Parts-of-Speech will help. Listen.

Present Tense

I am an Englishman merry and bold,
Thou art a foreigner out in the cold,
He is a beggar-man hungry and old;
We are not happy to see you out there,
You are too snug and warm ever to care,
They are at home with us now, I declare."

"That will do," interrupted the Judge; "we do not want to hear any more today. Another day I shall want to know what you mean by calling the verses *Present Tense*, *Past Tense*, and *Future Tense*—why you have just six of your words in each tense—" and whether other verbs can be *conjugated* in the same way."

"I can answer at once that they can, my lord," said Dr. Verb. "Indeed, very few verbs change as much as the verb *to be*, so that they are all easier to *conjugate*; as, *I have, thou hast, he has; we have, you have, they have. I live, thou livest, he lives; we live, you live, they live.*"

"Enough for today, Dr. Verb," interrupted the Judge once more; "we will hear about them next time. Meanwhile, as we shall have further examination of this verb *to be*, I should like my friends in Schoolroom Shire to make a copy of it, to bring with them. I shall also request them to find out all the verbs in the following verses:"

"Sit to your task," a father said,
　"Nor play nor trifle, laugh nor talk,
And when your lesson well is read,
　You all shall have a pleasant walk."

He left the room, the boys sat still,
　Each gravely bent upon his task,
But soon the youngest, little Will,
　Of fun and nonsense chose to ask.

"My ball is lost," the prattler cried,
　"Have either of you seen my ball?"
"Pray mind your book," young Charles replied.
　"Your noisy words disturb us all."

The court then rose.

Chapter 9
Dr. Verb's Three Tenses and Number and Person

NOW, Dr. Verb," said Judge Grammar, the next day, "we have well examined this that you call your 'Song of the verb To be.' "

"Conjugation, my lord, if you like," said Dr. Verb, bowing.

"I *do* like, certainly," replied the Judge. "Conjugation is a much better word than *song*—longer and more respectable, and in every way. more suited to Grammar Land. Con-ju-ga-tion—this conjugation of the verb 'to be.' We require you to explain it."

"With pleasure, my lord. You see, it is divided into three verses."

"Verses!" exclaimed Serjeant Parsing. "You know it is not to be called a song, Dr. Verb."

"Quite so, quite so," said Dr. Verb, bowing again. "Well, Tenses, then. It is divided into three tenses, the Present Tense, the Past Tense, and the Future Tense, which mean the present time, the past time, and the future time; and your lordship knows that all time must be either present time, or past time, or future time. Just as when you are reading a book. There is the part you have read, that is the past; the part you are going to read, that is the future; and the part you are reading now, that is the present."

"We understand," said Judge Grammar; "but pray explain why you divide your *verbs* into these three parts."

"To show how my verbs change when they have to mark the present, past, or future time. You see, the verb 'to be' takes *am* for the present, *was* for the past, and adds on *will* or *shall* for the future. *I am* in the present time talking to your lordship. *I was* in the past time talking to your lordship. *I shall be* in the future time talking to your lordship."

"Indeed, I hope not," cried the Judge, putting his hands to his ears. "Pray do not go on forever talking to me. I have heard quite enough of your voice already. Step back, and allow Mr. Pronoun to take your place, and explain the rest of the conjugation to us."

"Allow me to say one thing more," said Dr, Verb. "Please, Mr. Parsing, whenever you see a *will* or *shall*, or any other little verb put in to show the time, will you remember that it is only a little helping verb, used to make up the tense of some other verb, and therefore to be counted in with that, and not taken alone."

"Just give an example of what you mean," said Serjeant Parsing; "I do not quite understand."

"I mean to say that when you see 'he will go,' you must take *will go* as part of the verb *to go*; and when you see a*m coming, was dancing, has eaten, had fought,* you must take them as parts of the verbs to come, to dance, to eat, to fight. The first words, *am, was, has, had, are* very good and respectable words by themselves, of course; but when they are used with another verb, they are never offended if you just take them as part of that other verb."

"Thank you. I will remember," said Serjeant Parsing, laughing. "Now please to stand back, and allow Mr. Pronoun to answer. Mr. Pronoun, pray why do you use these particular six words, *I, thou, he, we, you,* and *they,* to make up Dr. Verb's tenses?"

"I use *I* and *we,*" answered Pronoun, "to stand for the first person; *thou* and *you* to stand for the second person; and *he* and *they* to stand for the third person."

"What do you mean by the first person?" asked Serjeant Parsing.

"My lord," answered Mr. Pronoun, turning to Judge Grammar, "may I ask you who is the first person in Grammar Land?"

"*I* am, of course," answered the Judge.

"That is what I find all my friends answer," said Pronoun. "When I ask them who is the most important, the first person in the world to them, they say *I am*; so my little *I* stands for the person who is speaking about himself, and I call it the *first* person."

"Then who is the *second* person?" asked the Judge.

"*You* are, my lord," answered Pronoun, bowing politely.

"You said just now that *I* was the *first* person," said the Judge.

"Yes, my lord," replied Mr. Pronoun, putting his hand on his breast; "*I* first, and *you* second."

"But it ought to be *I* first, and *you* second," said the Judge, angrily.

"That is exactly what I said, my lord," repeated Pronoun. "*I* first, and *you* second."

The Judge was getting so angry, that Pronoun's friends began to tremble for his head, when suddenly Dr. Syntax rose and said: "The first person is always the person speaking, and the second is the person spoken to. Let every one in the court say! '*I am* the first,' and we shall all be right, and all satisfied."

"*I* first, *we* first," they all shouted; "and *you, you, you,* only the second."

The noise was tremendous, and the Judge, finding himself only one against a number, thought he had better turn the subject; and clapping his hands loudly, to call for silence, he called out:

"But if we are all firsts and seconds, pray where is the third person to go?"

"Oh, the third person," said Pronoun, contemptuously, "is only the one we are talking about. He may not be here, so it cannot matter if we call him only the third person."

"And what is the use of your having pronouns to stand for all these three persons in Dr. Verb's tenses?" asked Serjeant Parsing.

"Dr. Verb and I agree together to alter our words according to the person they represent," said Mr. Pronoun.

"When my pronoun is in the first person, Dr. Verb has to make his verb in the first person too. He has to say *am* when I have put *I*, and *are* when I have put *we*. *I is*, or *we art*, would make Dr. Syntax there very angry."

"And he would be rightly angry," replied the Judge. "You know that very well."

"Oh, I am not complaining, my lord," answered Pronoun; "I was merely stating a fact. Of course I am rather pleased than otherwise that Dr. Verb should have to alter his words to make them agree with mine. My pronouns show the person (that is why, you know, they are called personal pronouns), and then Dr. Verb has to make his words agree with them."

"Very fine!" remarked Serjeant Parsing, "But tell us, Mr. Pronoun, why, when there are only three different persons, you should have six different pronouns in each tense?"

"Three of them are for the singular number, standing for only one —*I, thou, he*," replied Pronoun; "and the other three are for the plural number, standing for as many as you like—*we, you*, and *they*."

"Singular number only one, *I, thou, he*; plural number more than one, *we, you, they;*— that is it, is it not, Mr. Pronoun?" asked Serjeant Parsing.

"Yes, sir," replied Pronoun, "that is it exactly; I could not have explained it better myself. And whatever number the pronoun is, that the verb must be also."

"You mean that when the pronoun only stands for one thing or person, then both it and the verb that comes after it are said to be in the singular number: is it not so?" said Serjeant Parsing.

"Quite so, Mr. Parsing," said Pronoun, delighted; "the verb has to agree with the pronoun in number, just as it has to do in person. If my pronoun stands for only one, then it and the verb are called singular number; but if my pronoun stands for more than one thing, then it and the verb are said to be in the plural number. You quite understand me, I see, my dear Mr. Parsing, and I am sure you will take care to see that the verb always agrees with me in number and person."

"Whenever it is proper that it should," replied Serjeant Parsing, gravely.

"But it ought always to agree with my words when we are conjugating a verb together," said Pronoun, eagerly; "that is the very reason why it is useful to conjugate verbs. In every tense you have the first person, second person, and third person in the singular number; and the first person, second person, and third person in the plural number; and then you see how the verb alters each time to agree with the pronoun."

"It does not alter every time," put in Dr. Verb; "in some tenses it hardly alters at all. Just listen,—'I had, thou hadst, he had, we had, you had, they had; I lived, thou livedst, he lived, we lived, you lived, they lived; I sang, thou sangest, he sang, we sang, you sang, they sang; I rang, thou rangest, he rang, we rang, you rang; they rang.'"

"That will do, that will do, Dr. Verb," cried the Judge. "We have had your talking in the past tense, we do not want it in the present tense, and if we should happen to require it in the future tense, we will let you know another time. Instead of talking here, you had much better go to Schoolroom Shire, and help the people there to write out the present, past, and future tenses of the verbs you have mentioned—*to have, to live, to sing, to ring;* and show them how the words alter, not only to mark the different times, but to agree with Mr. Pronoun's words in number and person."

"I shall be most happy, my lord," said Dr. Verb," but Mr. Pronoun must come too, to help me."

"With great pleasure, my dear Doctor," said Mr. Pronoun, gaily. "There is no one in Grammar Land I can work with so easily as you, because you agree with me so beautifully."

Then, bowing to the Judge, he and Dr. Verb walked out of the court, arm-in-arm, humming the present tense of the verb *to be,* and the Schoolroom Shire people, with their help, easily wrote out the four verbs mentioned, *to have, to live, to sing,* and *to ring.*

Chapter 10
Serjeant Parsing in Schoolroom Shire Again

BEFORE the court met again, Serjeant Parsing paid another visit to Schoolroom Shire.

"My dear young friends," he said, "will you kindly get your slates, and divide them into four parts, writing at the top of each part, the name of Mr. Noun, Mr. Pronoun, Mr, Adjective, and Dr. Verb. Then cut off two corners somewhere, for little ragged Article and Interjection.

Then listen to the following story (next page), and when any word that you know is read out, give a mark to the Part-of-Speech to whom it belongs. If you come to an adjective-pronoun, of course you must put a little man astride between Mr. Pronoun's ground and Mr. Adjective's; and whenever you come to a verb, please to say whether it is in the present, past, or future tense. When you have done, we will count up, and see which Part-of-Speech has gained the most marks.

This is the story:

The Two Neighbors

A man lived by his labor; and as he had strong arms and a brave heart, he supported, easily, his wife, his little children, and himself.

But a famine came upon the land, and work failed.

The man spent all the money which he had saved, until he had not a penny to buy food for his children.

Then he went to a rich neighbor, and said: "My little children are crying for food, and I have no bread to give them. Help me."

And the rich man said:

"I am a just man; I always pay my debts; but I owe you no money. Go! I cannot give you charity."

Then the poor man went to another neighbor, almost as poor as himself.

"Give me food for my little children," he said.

"Brother," said the poorer neighbor, "we have not much ourselves, but you shall share with us as long as a crust of bread remains."

Then they divided between them the little food that was left, and that food lasted until the hard times had passed.

Chapter 11
The Nominative Case

THE next day, Dr. Verb came bustling into the court, looking very cross, and calling out loudly for justice.

"What is the matter?" asked the Judge; "state your case quietly."

It is not *my* case, it is Pronoun's case, that is the matter," answered Dr. Verb; "though I do not say it is his fault. We should get on very well if people would only mind their own business."

"If you will not tell me the state of the case clearly, I cannot help you," said the Judge.

"Well, my lord, if you will listen for a minute, I will try to explain it, so that every one can understand. As you know very well, I am constantly agreeing with Mr. Pronoun. I showed you how I alter to suit his number and person, and it is only fair that he should alter sometimes to suit me. I only agree with him when he is in the "Nominative Case."

At the words "Nominative Case" there was a real cry of horror from nearly every one in court. You might have thought they had all turned into interjections, they made such a fuss.

"Nominative Case!" cried Noun; "shame, shame!"

"Shameful! awful! shocking!" cried Adjective.

"Fie! fie! fie!" cried Interjection, and turned three times over head and heels.

"Pray do not use such words, Dr. Verb," said Judge Grammar, "but tell us what you mean."

"Really, my lord," said Dr. Verb, "I did not mean any harm. Nominative is not such a *very* long word, that people should make such a fuss about it. I am sure the ladies and gentlemen of the jury will not be angry at my using it."

"That depends on how you explain it," said the Judge; "What does it mean?"

"It means the person or thing that *is* or *does* whatever my verb says about him. *The cat purrs.* It is the cat that does what the verb mentions. You have only to put 'who' before the verb in any sentence, and the answer will give you the Nominative. 'Who purrs?' The answer is the *cat*, so *cat* is the nominative to the verb *purrs*. That is the way that *I* find out whom I am to make my verb agree with."

"Is that *your* way, Brother Parsing?" asked the Judge.

"Yes, my lord," answered Serjeant Parsing, "that is my way, and therefore, of course, it is the best way. My way is always the best way. Now there is a sentence all ready for you: *My way is always the best way.* I'll find the nominative before you can dot an i. '*What* is always the best way?' Answer, *my way* is always the best way; so *my way* is the Nominative."

"But you asked 'what?' not 'who?' there, Brother Parsing," remarked the Judge.

"Because *way* is a thing, not a person, my lord. When we are talking of a thing, then we ask 'what?' instead of 'who?' If you said 'the pudding is boiling in the pot,' I should say '*what* is boiling?' not '*who* is boiling?' for I should hope you would not be boiling a *person* in a pot, unless you were the giant in Jack and the Beanstalk."

"Fi! fo! fum!" said Interjection, standing on his head, and clapping his heels together.

"Silence, sir!" cried the Judge. "Brother Parsing, please not to talk about giants till we have done with the Nominative Case. Has any gentleman anything more to explain about it?"

"Please, my lord," said Pronoun, "Dr. Verb complains that he has to agree with me when I am in the Nominative Case. But he has to agree with Mr. Noun just as much. It is no matter what part of speech stands as the Nominative in a sentence, Dr. Verb must agree with it; so he need not grumble at me more than at any one else."

"I am not grumbling at you—," Dr. Verb began.

"Wait a minute, Dr. Verb," interrupted the Judge; "let us first fully understand this case. You say there is a verb in every sentence?"

"Certainly, my lord," said Verb.

"And there is a Nominative in every sentence?"

"Exactly so, my lord," answered Serjeant Parsing.

"And this Nominative may be a noun or a pronoun?" continued the Judge.

"It may, my lord," chimed in both Mr. Noun and Mr. Pronoun.

"And this verb must agree with this Nominative, whether it likes or not?" asked the Judge.

At that question Dr. Syntax suddenly started up like a jack-in-the-box, and standing bolt upright, said, "A verb must agree with its Nominative case in number and person. A verb must agree with its Nominative case in number and person;" and then sank down again.

"Ah!" said the Judge. "Very good. So you see, Dr. Verb, when you have a sentence like 'ducks swim in ponds,' you are first to find your own word swim, then to put *who* or *what* before it—'who swim?' or 'what swim?' The answer will be ducks, the Nominative. Then you are to be sure that the verb agrees with it. You must say 'ducks swim,' not 'ducks swims;' and as ducks is the third person and plural number, swim will be third person and plural number too."

"Please, my lord," said Pronoun," when I am Nominative you need very seldom take the trouble to ask any question to find out the Nominative, for most of my words show at once what they are in. *I, thou, he, she, we,* and *they* will never allow themselves to be used except as Nominatives. They were born Nominatives, they say, and will not degrade themselves by being anything else. They are rather angry with *you* for letting people use *him* in any way they like, but he is a good-natured little fellow, and does not mind any more about the case than he does about being called singular when he is really plural. But *I, thou, he, she, we,* and *they,* are exceedingly particular, and always are and will be Nominatives, so you need not ask any question when you see one of them in a sentence."

"You may just as well make it a rule to ask 'who?' or ' what?' in every sentence, to find the Nominative," said Serjeant Parsing. "It is such an easy way of finding the case that a baby in arms could understand it."

"Tut! tut! tut! tut!" laughed Interjection again.

"Oh! be quiet, do!" said Serjeant Parsing; "and, my lord, if the ladies and gentle-men of Schoolroom Shire like to find out the Nominatives in these verses—"

"Yes," said the Judge; "hand them up, brother. No, do not begin again, Dr. Verb; no more complaints today. And remember, friends, that in these lines every verb must have a Nominative, unless there is a little *to* before the verb. Then it has none—it does not agree with anything. And remember, too, that every noun or pronoun that is in the Nominative case is to get an extra mark on your slates. I wish you good morning, gentlemen."

So saying, the Judge rose. The verses were handed to the people of Schoolroom Shire, and the court was cleared.

Serjeant Parsing's Verses

The hen guards well her little chicks,
　The useful cow is meek:
The beaver builds with mud and sticks,
　The lapwing loves to squeak.

In Germany they hunt the boar,
　The bee brings honey home;
The ant lays up a winter store,
　The bear loves honeycomb.

I lost my poor little doll, dears,
　As I played on the heath one day;
And I cried for her more than a week, dears,
　But I never could find where she lay.

The maidens laughed, the children played,
　The boys cut many capers.
While aunt was lecturing the maid,
　And uncle read the papers.

Chapter 12
Adverb

NOW DR. VERB," said Judge Grammar, next day, "I am ready to hear what is your great complaint against Pronoun."

"Why, my lord, when he is in the Objective Case—"

"I object, I object!" exclaimed the Judge, while a general murmur of disapproval ran through the court. "No, no, we have had enough with the Nominative Case; we will not have another case brought in. You ought to be ashamed of yourself, sir, to keep us listening to your nonsense about an Objective case, while your devoted friend Adverb is waiting to be heard. Sit down, and let Adverb speak."

"Devoted friend!" muttered Dr. Verb, as he obeyed. "I am sure I often wish he would leave me alone. He sticks on to me so tight sometimes, that we look like one instead of two, and he is a good weight to carry. Besides, he is always teasing by asking *why*, and *when*, and *how* everything is done. Friend, indeed!"

But Adverb did not hear what Dr. Verb was muttering. He came forward, bowing politely, and rubbing his hands together, as if he were washing them.

"*Very much* obliged, indeed," he said, smoothly; "*very* kind of my friend Dr. Verb to give way to me! *So* like him!"

"You seem to be fonder of him than he is of you," remarked the Judge. "Pray, why do you follow him so closely?"

"I like to hear what he says, and to point out to others *how exceedingly well* he speaks," answered Adverb.

"He is always exaggerating my words," grumbled Dr. Verb. "If I say I like anything, Adverb puts in *very much indeed*, or *extremely well*, or some such silly words; or, if he is in a bad temper, then he flatly contradicts me, and says, *no*, or *not*, or *never*. If I say *will*, he adds *not*, and makes it *will not*; if I say *can*, he makes it *cannot*, even sticking his word on to mine as if it were part of it. Sometimes he does worse. He actually dares to alter my word after he has stuck his tail on to it, and so he makes *will not* into *won't*, *cannot* into *can't*, *shall not* into *sha'n't*, and so on. The *wo'*, and *ca'*, and *sha'*, is all he has left me, and the *n't* is his."

"Has he always treated you in this way?" asked the Judge.

"As long as I can remember, my lord," answered Dr. Verb. "That is why, when we were at school together, the boys called him *Adverb*, because he was always *adding* his words on to mine. And he has kept the name ever since."

"Your lordship must remember," remarked Adverb, in a mild tone, still rubbing his hands very smoothly together, "that Dr. Verb is *rather* out of temper this morning, and is, *perhaps, not quite* just. For *indeed* it is a fact that I make his words *much more* useful than they *otherwise* would be. Besides, I treat Mr. Adjective in *much* the same way, and he does not complain."

"It is quite true," remarked Adjective, coming forward, delighted to get a chance of using his tongue; "it is quite true that Adverb has his word to say about me, just as much as about Dr. Verb. He is always putting *very, quite, more, most*, and words of that sort, before my adjectives, and exaggerating them: as, *very* beautiful, *quite* charming, *more* obstinate, *most* provoking, and I do not complain of him for that. But one thing I do complain of, my lord, and that is, that Adverb will take my words, right good adjectives, stick a *ly* on to them, and call them his adverbs. For instance, he takes *bright*, puts *ly* to it, and makes it *brightly*; he takes *bad*, and makes it *badly*; *nice*, and makes it *nicely*, *beautiful*, and makes it *beautifully*."

Judge Grammar at this held up his forefinger, and solemnly shook his head, till he nearly shook his wig off.

"Mr. Adjective, Mr. Adjective!" he said, "I am surprised at you. You complain of Adverb for doing the very thing that you do yourself. We all know that you keep your pockets full of tails ready to stick on to your neighbors' words—*ful, ous, able, like, ly,* and plenty more, and you use them as often as you can with other people's words. But when Adverb uses his one little *ly* with *your* words, then you are up in arms directly. And yet you know very well that according to the laws of Grammar Land every Part-of-Speech may make as many new words out of old ones as he likes, and is to be praised, not blamed, for it. Adverb may put his *ly* on to as many of your words as he can, and you have no right to find fault. I wonder at both you and Dr. Verb. You ought to agree with Adverb better."

"We none of us agree with him," remarked Pronoun, "nor he with us."

"He certainly has no number, or person, or case," replied the Judge; "but he is none the worse for that. He gives Serjeant Parsing less trouble than some of you. What did you say about asking questions, Adverb?"

"I teach the game of *how, when,* and *where,*" replied Adverb; "*how, when,* and *where,* are all my words, and so are the answers to them.

> How do you like it? pray you tell?
> *Not too bad, extremely well.*
> Why do you like it, tell me *when?*
> *Today, tomorrow, now,* and *then.*
> *Where* do you like it, answer fair?
> *Here* and *there* and *everywhere.*

All these words that answer *how, when,* and *where,* are mine," continued Adverb, "and so are the forfeit words *yes, no,* or *nay.*"

"Ah! but *black, white,* and *gray* are mine," said Adjective, interrupting; "and please, your lordship, you were mistaken in saying that Adverb has only one tail, *ly,* to put on to other people's words. What do you think of *upwards, downwards, homeward, forward?*"

"Yes, they are certainly adverbs," said the Judge, "and you might say that *wards* and *ward* are the tails he has added on to *up, down, home, for*; but these words are not yours, Mr. Adjective, so you have no right to interfere."

"Well, my lord," replied Adjective, "at any rate I have a right to speak about *once, twice, thrice,* for Adverb has stolen them from my *one, two, three.*"

"*Once, twice, thrice,*" repeated the Judge; "is that all?"

"He has not got a word for four times," answered Adjective; "*once, twice, thrice,* and *away,* is all that he can say,"

"Then I think," said the Judge, "that you ought to be ashamed to grudge them to him, when you have *one, two, three,* and as many more as you can count; besides *first, second, third, fourth,* and all that list. I do not like such greedy ways, and as a punishment, I order you to hand up a list of adjectives to be turned into adverbs. Our friends may take them to Schoolroom Shire and put a *ly* to each of them; then they will be adverbs, and will answer to one of Adverb's questions, *how, when,* or *where.*"

This is the list Mr. Adjective made out.

quick	*sudden*	*pretty*
bright	*late*	*dainty*
soft	*punctual*	*funny*
strong	*regular*	*free*
distinct	*sly*	*happy*
clear	*cunning*	*awful*
neat	*false*	
sharp	*true*	

Chapter 13

Preposition

O, *from, of, for, over, under, on, near, at, by, in, among, before, behind, up, down*—Pray, who is the owner of all these little creatures?" said Judge Grammar, the next clay. "Mr . Noun, are they yours?"

"No, indeed, my lord," answered Mr. Noun, "they are not the names of any one or anything that I ever heard of."

"Dr. Verb, are they yours?"

"I should not object to having them, my lord," answered Dr. Verb, "if I could do anything with them; but they seem to me neither *to be* nor *to do*, nor *to suffer* any—"

"That will do," interrupted the Judge, afraid that Dr. Verb was beginning one of his long speeches. "Mr. Adjective, do you claim them?"

"They do not qualify anything, my lord," answered Adjective; "indeed, they seem to me *poor, useless, silly, little*—"

"We do not want you to qualify them, thank you," said the Judge, "but to tell us if they are yours. Article, we know, has only *a* or *an* and *the*, so they cannot be his. Mr. Pronoun, do they belong to you?"

"No, my lord," answered Pronoun. "As Mr. Noun has nothing to say to them, neither have I. They do not stand instead of any name."

"Well," said the Judge, "we know they do not belong to that tiresome little Interjection. Are they yours, Adverb?"

"I should be *extremely* glad to have them, my lord," answered Adverb, smoothly washing his hands, as usual. "I have no doubt I could make them *exceedingly* useful—"

"That is not what I asked," said the Judge: "are they yours?"

"I cannot say they are *exactly* mine," said Adverb; "but—"

"That is all we want to know," interrupted the Judge. Then raising his voice, he continued: "If there is any one in this court to whom these words, 'to, from, of, for,' etc., do belong, let him come forward."

At these words, a sharp, dapper little fellow stepped forward, and looking around the court with a triumphant air, exclaimed, "They belong to me."

"And who are you?"

"Preposition, my lord. My position is just before a noun or pronoun. My words point out to them their proper position. I keep them in order."

"You keep them in order?" said Judge Grammar, looking down at him through his spectacles; "how can a little mite like you keep Mr. Noun in order?"

"Little or big, my lord, that's what I do," said Preposition. "I settle the position of every one and every thing, and show whether they are to be *on* or *under*, *to* or *from*, *up* or *down*."

"*Kindly* forgive me for interrupting you," said Adverb, coming forward. "I *really* must remark that *up* and *down* are my words."

"How do you make out that?" asked the Judge.

"I will show you *directly*, my lord," answered Adverb.

"By the help of my questions *how*, *when*, and *where*, which, you know, I alone can answer. If you say, 'sit up,' I ask, *how* am I to sit?' The answer is, '*up*.' 'Lie down; '*how* am I to lie?' The answer is, '*down*,' Up and *down*, therefore, answer to my question *how*, and are mine."

"Stop a minute," said Preposition. "I also can answer to your favorite questions *how*, *when*, and *where*. Listen:

How do you like it? tell me true.
Made *of* sugar, dressed *in* blue,
When do you like it? answer me.
At my dinner; *after* tea,
"*Where* do you like it? say, if you're able.
On my lap or *under* the table?"

"*Really,*" said Adverb, smiling politely, "that is *very* cleverly done. But allow me to make *just* one remark. You have not answered one single question without the help of some other part of speech. Mr. Noun has helped you with 'sugar,' 'dinner,' 'tea,' 'lap,' 'table;' Mr. Adjective lent you 'blue;' Mr. Pronoun, 'my;' and so on. Now I, without any help, answer the questions quite alone."

"You cannot expect a little fellow like me to stand quite alone," said Preposition; "I don't pretend to do it. I told you at first that my right position is before a noun or pronoun, or some such word. All I mean is that I help to answer the questions, and that neither Mr. Noun nor Mr. Pronoun could answer them without me."

"Is that true, Brother Parsing?" asked the Judge.

"Quite true, my lord," answered the learned Serjeant. "When I find the questions 'how?' 'when?' or 'where?' answered by one word alone, I put that word down to Adverb. But when I find them answered by Mr. Noun or Mr. Pronoun, helped by another little word, then I know that that other little word belongs to Preposition."

"Yes, my lord," continued Preposition; "so if you say '*up* a ladder' or' '*down* a hill,' *up* and *down* are mine; they show your position on the *ladder* or the *hill*; they are the little prepositions put before Mr. Noun's words *ladder* and *hill*. But, of course, if you were to ask how I am to step *up* or *down*? then Adverb could call up and down *adverbs*, because they are added on to the verb 'step,' and they have nothing to do with a noun or a pronoun.

"*Precisely,*" said Adverb; "my friend Preposition is *perfectly* correct. I *immensely* admire my young friend, although he does not move in *quite so* select a circle as myself."

"Don't I?" said Preposition, with a knowing little nod. "I think Mr. Noun quite as good company as Dr. Verb, any day. Besides, even grand Dr. Verb is glad enough to have my little *to* to put before his verbs. When he makes up his 'songs,' as he calls them, he always puts my little *to* before the name at the top. He is glad enough to have it to point out his verbs, and does not despise me at all, though I do not stick on to him like a leech, as some people do," and Preposition nodded his head very fast a great many times at Adverb.

"Dr. Verb does not agree with you, though," remarked Pronoun, quietly.

"No," said Preposition, "I do not alter for him, nor he for me. But he does not agree with Adverb either. Poor Adverb agrees with nobody, and nobody agrees with him; and he, poor fellow! cannot govern anybody, either. Now I govern every noun or pronoun that I come before, for I put them in the Objective Case."

"I object," cried the Judge. "I will not have that word brought into court. I said so before, and I say so again. Nominative Case is bad enough, but Objective Case is enough to turn a brown wig gray in a single night. Break up the court! Critics, clear the room!"

And Judge Grammar rose hastily from his seat, and stalked angrily out, while all the Parts-of-Speech stood looking speechlessly at each other till the policemen came, bundled them all out, and locked the doors behind them.

In spite of the hurry, however, Serjeant Parsing managed to hand up to the people of Schoolroom Shire the following verses, begging the ladies and gentlemen there to find out all the prepositions in them, and to count how many lines there are in which Preposition has nothing to say.

The Fairy Ring

Beside a bluebell on the heath,
  Among the purple heather,
A fairy lived, and crept beneath
  The leaves in windy weather.

She drank the dewdrops from the stalk,
  See peeped into the flower;
And then she went to take a walk,
  Or ride for half-an-hour.

She rode upon a cricket's back,
  She came before the Queen,
The fairy Queen, with all her court,
  Within the forest green.

They had a dance upon the grass,
  Till larks began to sing;
And where they danced, as all may know
  They left a fairy-ring.

Oh, pretty fairies! why not stay,
  That we at you may peep?
Why will you only dance and play
  When we are fast asleep?

Chapter 14
Prepositions Govern The Objective Case

When the Parts-of-Speech found themselves so suddenly turned out of the court, they collected in a group before the door, and looked at each other in astonishment."

"Here is a pretty thing!" said Mr. Noun, indignantly. "Fine way to treat us, indeed!"

"And after all, I only said what is true," said Preposition. "I do put every noun or pronoun that comes after my words in the Objective Case, do I not, Dr. Syntax?"

"Prepositions govern the Objective Case," said Dr. Syntax, in his usual monotonous voice; then lifting his spectacles, he twisted his head round to look at Preposition, and actually deigned to explain his words by saying: "Whatever noun or pronoun a preposition is placed before and refers to, must be in the Objective Case."

"Speak to him," murmured Serjeant Parsing, as if he were talking to himself: "*him*, a pronoun, objective case, governed by the preposition *to*."

"Mr. Pronoun, you hear that!" exclaimed Mr. Noun. "This little Preposition is said to govern us, you and me, in the Objective Case. Very impertinent, on my word!"

"On my word!" again muttered Serjeant Parsing. "Word, a noun, Objective Case, governed by the preposition *on*."

"However, it does not matter to me," continued Mr. Noun, without taking any notice of Serjeant Parsing. "It will make no difference to me;" and he turned away, with his hands in his pockets, and began to whistle a tune.

"It does matter to me, though," said Pronoun, "for I have to alter my words according to the case they are in. *I* is only in the nominative case, *me* in the objective; *we* is nominative, *us* objective; *he* nominative, *him* objective, and so on. You cannot say 'look at *I*;' you must say 'look at *me*.'"

"Look at me," echoed Serjeant Parsing, in the same quiet tone: "*me*, Objective Case, governed by the preposition *at*."

"Quite so," continued Pronoun, turning to Serjeant Parsing. "I am objective there, I cannot help it; I must be objective after a preposition."

"Yes," said Serjeant Parsing, aloud, "and it is very convenient for me that you must. It often helps me to find out whether a word is really a preposition or no. I just try whether it wants *I* or *me* after it. Take *when* or *if*, for instance. You can say, when *I* go, if *I* were; so *when* and *if* are not prepositions. But you cannot say 'for *I*,' or 'from *I*;' you must have the Objective Case, and say for *me*, from *me*, so *for* and *from* are prepositions governing the Objective Case."

"You had better take care," said Preposition; "you keep on saying Objective Case, and if you say it before Judge Grammar, you know you will get us all into trouble again."

"Oh, never fear," said Serjeant Parsing; "the Judge will listen to us patiently enough, next time. Besides, he must hear about Objective Case, whether he likes it or no, because the prize will partly depend upon it."

"The prize! what prize?" cried every one.

"Listen. There is to be a grand trial or examination soon. All the Schoolroom Shire children are to be invited, and all you Parts-of-Speech are to make up a story between you. You will each get a mark for every word you give, and whoever gets the most marks will get—"

"Yes, what? what will he get?" they all cried out eagerly.

"Ah! that is a secret. What I want to tell you is, that any word that governs another will get an extra mark. For instance, when I say 'Listen to me,' the preposition *to* puts *me* in the Objective Case, so *to* will get an extra mark."

"That is splendid!" cried little Preposition, clapping his hands and jumping about for joy. "I always govern a noun or pronoun in the Objective Case, so I shall get two marks every time I come in."

"Not quite so sure," interrupted Dr. Verb. "Sometimes you come before a verb, *to* eat, *to* sleep, *to* fly, and then you can only get one mark, for you do not govern me, my little dear, seeing that verbs do not have a case at all."

"Ah, but you have to agree with your Nominative Case, Dr. Verb," said Pronoun; "so I suppose, when I am nominative, I shall have an extra mark, for I might be said to govern you in a sort of way."

"No, no," said Serjeant Parsing, putting in his word, "you are not said to govern Dr. Verb; he agrees with you, that is all; but the Nominative Case, being a very honorable one, will always get two marks."

"Then," said Mr. Noun, suddenly stopping his whistling and taking an interest in the conversation, "I am of course to get two marks for every noun in the Nominative Case?"

"Certainly," answered Serjeant Parsing.

"And in the Objective Case also?" asked Mr. Noun.

"No, no," said Serjeant Parsing, laughing; "that would be too much of a good thing, since your words are nearly always either nominative or objective. No, no; on the contrary, the Objective Case, being governed by other words (even such little trifles as prepositions), is not considered at all an honorable case, and therefore will not only give a noun or pronoun no extra marks, but will take away one of those it already has. For instance, if I am parsing 'Come to me,' and I give Mr. Pronoun a mark for *me*, I must strike out that mark as soon as I find that *me* is in the Objective Case, and must give it to Preposition for his little word *to*, which governs *me*."

Mr. Noun and Mr. Pronoun both looked very dismal at these tidings, and then Mr. Noun said:

"I hope no one else except Preposition can put me into the Objective Case."

"O yes, indeed, I can," cried Dr. Verb, bustling up, eagerly; but Serjeant Parsing stopped him.

"No, no, Dr; Verb," he said," we are not going to begin that question. No notice will be taken of any noun or pronoun's being in the Objective Case, unless it is governed by a preposition. That is the rule for this trial; another time, perhaps, your rights will be considered."

Serjeant Parsing then took the following lines to Schoolroom Shire, that every Objective Case governed by a preposition might be found out:

> Tom called for me, I went with him,
>> We climbed upon a rock;
> There over the sea we looked for thee,
>> Till seven of the clock.
> And then a white sail over the main,
>> Brought back our sailor-boy again.

Fill up the blanks with a noun or pronoun, and say whether it will be nominative or objective.

_____ went for a walk yesterday, _____ walked through a dark _____ under tall _____ ; suddenly, when _____ were in a very lonely _____ , _____ heard the steps of some _____ crashing through the _____ "What can it be?" _____ cried _____ stopped to listen; the _____ came nearer, two bright eyes gleamed at us through the _____ , and in another _____ out bounded, with a deep _____ that made echoes all round us, our own dear old _____ , who had broken his chain, escaped from the _____ , and had come out to look for _____ .

Chapter 15

Conjunction

"MY lord," said Serjeant Parsing, the next time that the court assembled, "I must beg for your assistance. I have here a story—a very excellent story, as it seems to me; but somehow or other it will not go right — it has what you might call a jerky sound—as if you were riding over a corduroy road in a cart without springs, and were trying to talk between the bumps. I have asked all the Parts-of-Speech that are in court to help me, but none of them can give me any assistance."

"Read the story aloud," said the Judge, "and let us hear it."

So Serjeant Parsing read—

The Eagle and the Raven

"An eagle pounced on a little lamb . . . . carried it off in his claws. A raven saw him fly . . . . thought he could do the same; . . . . he chose out the best . . . . biggest sheep of the flock, ... pounced down upon it; . . . . lo! . . . . behold! it was much too heavy . . . . it was much bigger . . . . himself, poor

Mr. Raven only got his claws entangled in the wool . . . . when he tried to fly away he found it impossible to get free . . . . he was struggling . . . . when the shepherd came . . . caught him . . . . put him in a cage."

"I see, I see," said the Judge, "you want some words to join your sentences together. Noun, Pronoun, Article, Adjective, Verb, Adverb, Preposition, none of these will do. I have only two other Parts-of-Speech left on my list: that tiresome Interjection, who is, of course, no use, and Con—"

"Conjunction? Here you are, my lord," said a bright cheery voice at the door, and Conjunction walked into court.

He had on a coat with brass buttons, and a cap like a railway guard's, with C. J. marked on the front. Under his arm he had a bundle of iron hooks or tools—at least what you would have thought were iron hooks or tools, if you had seen them down in Matter-of-fact-land, and had not known any better. They were really his words.

"You are late, sir," said the Judge, very sternly; "where have you been?"

"To tell you the truth, my lord," answered Conjunction, "I have been for a little holiday trip on the Grammar Land Railway. The fact is, my turn was so long in coming, and the last time I was here your lordship broke up the court in such a temp—"

"A what, sir?" interrupted the Judge, angrily.

"A hurry, my lord,—in such a hurry, that I did not think we should meet again for some time; and so I just amused myself by a trip on the railway, where I am so often at work."

"Very improper, indeed! "replied the Judge, "as if you were made to amuse yourself. Such a thing was never heard of before in Grammar Land. Ask Dr. Syntax whether conjunctions are used for amusement."

"Conjunctions are used to connect words or sentences," said Dr. Syntax, in his solemn unchanging voice, standing up to speak, and sinking down the moment he had finished.

"There!" said the Judge, "you hear what you are used for—to connect words or sentences—that is your work, and that is just what we have been wanting you for. You have kept the whole court waiting, while you have been taking a holiday, forsooth! Your very cap ought to shame you. Pray what does C. J. stand for?"

"Well, my lord, the folks in Matter-of-fact-land say that it stands for Clapham Junction, which is a big station down there, where a great many railways are joined together; and they say that I am the pointsman, who moves the rails and makes the trains run together, or apart, as the case may be; and I don't know but what thats as good a description of my work as the folks in Matter-of-fact-land could give. Only they ought to understand that our trains in Grammar Land are sentences, and my tools with which I join them together are my words—*and, but, if, also,* and so on. And here they are, Mr. Parsing, and heartily at your service, sir, if you like to make use of them;" and pulling the bundle from under his arm, Conjunction laid them down before Serjeant Parsing, with a bow.

"Thank you, my man," said Serjeant Parsing, "one at a time, if you please. I will read my story again, and do you hang up a word that will fit, whenever I stop for it."

So he read it again, and Conjunction put in the words as follows:

The Eagle and the Raven

"*An eagle pounced on a little lamb* and *carried it off in his claws. A raven saw him fly,* and *thought he could do the same; so he chose out the best* and *biggest sheep of the flock,* and *pounced down upon it;* but *lo!* and *behold! it was much too heavy,* for *it was much bigger* than *himself,* so *poor Mr. Raven only got his claws entangled in the wool,* and *when he tried to fly away, he found it impossible to get free;* and whilst *he was struggling, the shepherd came* and *caught him* and *put him in a cage.*"

Ah," said Judge Grammar, "yes, that is an improvement. I see, Conjunction, you have put in *and, so, but, than, for, whilst.* What other words have you?"

"I have *because,* my lord," answered Conjunction. "Mr. Adverb asks 'why?' but I answer 'because,' which is much more useful. Any one can ask 'why?' but it is only a fellow like me, that knows how things work, that can answer 'because.' "

"You need not boast," said the Judge; "you only join the trains together, you know; you do not make them. *Because* is only useful on account of what comes after it; it would not tell us much if it stood alone. But what others have you?"

"I have *if,* my lord; and though it is only a word of two letters, it makes a mighty difference many a time. How happy we should all be *if* we could get just what we want."

"Yes, yes, we know," said the Judge; " '*if* wishes were horses, beggars would ride;' but it is a very good thing they are not. Now, Conjunction, *if* you have any more words, let us hear them.

"Except that I sometimes use my neighbors' words as conjunctions, my lord," answered Conjunction, "I think I have told you pretty well all. Here is a packet I put together:

"If, because, and, so, that, or,
But, although, as, also, nor."

"One more question," said the Judge; "do you govern or agree with any of your neighbors?"

"Not I, my lord, I leave that for my betters. I am quite satisfied to join them together, and then leave them alone," answered Conjunction.

"Then that will do for today. Brother Parsing, be good enough to send the following story to Schoolroom Shire, and tell them to give Conjunction a place on their slates among the other Parts-of-Speech, and mark down all his words for him. When that is done, I shall have some good news to tell you."

The court then rose.

A Narrow Escape

A traveler in India one day strayed away from his companions, and went to sleep under a tree. When he awoke he saw, to his horror, the two bright eyes of a tiger, ready to spring upon him from a high bank. He leaped up to run away, but fell back again directly, for a large crocodile was coming towards him, with its great mouth open. He shut his eyes and waited in terror, for he heard the tiger spring. A tremendous noise followed; but he felt nothing. He opened his eyes, and lo! the tiger had sprung into the mouth of the crocodile; and while the two wild beasts were struggling, the traveler sprang up and ran away.

Chapter 16
Active Verbs Govern The Objective Case

AND now, gentlemen," said Judge Grammr, when next they were assembled. "But what is the matter, Dr. Verb? What is this about? he asked, interupting himself, for Dr. Verb had gone down on one knee before the Judge, and was holding out a paper to him.

"A petition, your lordship," said Dr. Verb, solemnly; "I beg for justice. No, Preposition, it is of no use to try to hold me back, and to whisper that his lordship will be very angry. You have had your rights given you, and I am going to claim mine. My lord, I beg for the right of an extra mark whenever any word of mine governs a noun or pronoun in the Objective Case."

At the words "Objective Case," every one in the court held his breath, expecting the Judge to burst into a rage; and certainly a sudden flush did overspread his face, and rise to the very roots of his wig. For a moment he sat silent with compressed lips, then lifting his head haughtily, he said:

"Do not apologize, Dr. Verb; I forgive you; but on one condition—that you show clearly and at once how to discover an Objective Case that is governed by a verb."

"Certainly, my lord," said Dr. Verb, joyfully; "it is the easiest thing in the world. Just as you have to ask the question, 'who?' or 'what?' *before* the verb, to find out the Nominative Case, so you must ask the question, 'whom?' or ' what?' *after* the verb, to find the Objective Case. For the nominative tells you who did the thing, and the objective tells you to whom the thing was done. Here is an example: 'Harry kicked the cat.' You ask, 'who kicked?' to find the nominative, and the answer is *Harry*. You ask, 'Harry kicked what?' to find the objective, and the answer is, *the cat*. Is that clear?"

"The cat would certainly object," muttered the Judge; but I suppose that is not why it is called objective, because if the verb had been *fed*, *cat* would have been objective all the same. Well, Brother Parsing," he continued aloud, "did Dr. Verb explain the matter clearly? Could you find out the objective in that way?"

"Certainly, my lord," answered Serjeant Parsing, readily. "I will give you an example to prove it. 'I ate my dinner.' I find the nominative by asking 'who ate?' answer: *I*. I find the objective by asking 'I ate what?' answer: *dinner*; and dinner is clearly the objective, for it was the object for which I sat down to eat."

"Must all verbs have an Objective Case after them?" asked the Judge.

"They cannot all govern the objective," Serjeant Parsing began, when he was interrupted by a solemn voice near him, as Dr. Syntax suddenly rose and said, "Active verbs govern the Objective Case; active verbs govern the Objective Case;" and then sat down again.

"I know what he means by that," said Dr. Verb, "Active verbs are those whose action passes on to some one or something else, as in the sentence, 'Harry kicked the cat,' the action of kicking passed on to the poor cat; and in 'I ate my dinner,' the action of eating passed on and consumed the dinner; so *kick* and *eat* are both active verbs, and govern an Objective Case."

"Well, then," said the Judge, "must all *active* verbs have an Objective Case?"

"They should have one, my lord, if you want to make the sentence complete. You must give them an *object* for their activity. Every active boy can do *something*, though it may not be Latin, and the same with every active verb. If it *is* an active verb you can always put *some one* or *something* after it; as to *eat* something, *drink* something, *see* something, *love* somebody."

"And if the verb is not active?" asked the Judge.

"Then it usually has a preposition between it and the noun or pronoun after it, as, 'I think *of* you.' And the preposition gets all the honor and glory of governing the Objective Case, and gets an extra mark besides."

"Well," said the Judge, "you have explained it pretty clearly. I suppose I must allow you an extra mark for every verb that governs an Objective Case."

"But, please, my lord," said Mr. Noun, coming forward, "I suppose that Pronoun and I are not to lose a mark for every word of ours that is governed by a verb. That would be very hard."

"No, no," said the Judge. "There is no dishonor in being governed by an active verb; it is only when you allow yourselves to be governed by a little mite like Preposition, that you are to lose a mark."

"Allow ourselves to be governed," muttered Mr. Noun. "As if we could help it, when Dr. Syntax has once made the rule."

"Brother Parsing," said the Judge, "let us have a sentence to 'parse,' as you call it, that we may see clearly how it is done."

"Certainly, my lord," said Serjeant Parsing, turning over his papers. "Here is an excellent sentence, or rather, I should say, two sentences, for there are two verbs: 'Jack suddenly gave a loud cry, for lo! a tiger appeared before him.' Now let each Part-of-Speech claim the word as I read it. *Jack*."

"Mine" said Mr. Noun. "*Jack* is a proper noun."

"*Suddenly*" said Serjeant Parsing.

"Certainly *suddenly* is mine," said Adverb, smoothly.

"*Gave*," said Serjeant Parsing.

"*Gave* is mine," said Dr. Verb, "and it agrees with its nominative, *Jack*. For 'who gave?' *Jack* gave, so *Jack* is the nominative: and please, Mr. Noun, what number and person is *Jack*, for *gave* must be the same?"

"*Jack* is singular number, of course," said Mr. Noun, "for there is only one Jack mentioned; and it is third person, for you are talking about him, not *to* him, and, of course, he is not talking of himself: my words never do that."

"Oh," said Dr. Verb, then *Jack* is third person singular, is he? then *gave* is third person singular, too; and it is an active verb, and has an Objective Case. 'Jack gave what?' a *cry*—*cry* is the objective, governed by the active verb gave; so an extra mark for me, please Serjeant Parsing."

"All right," said the learned Serjeant. "*A* is the next word."

"Mine," said little Article.

"*Loud*," continued Serjeant Parsing.

"*Loud* is mine," said Adjective; "it qualifies cry—tells what sort of a cry he gave."

"Good," said Serjeant Parsing; "now, *cry*."

"Mine," said Mr. Noun; "a common noun this time, and Objective Case; but it does not lose a mark, as it is governed by an active verb, not by a preposition."

"*For*," continued Serjeant Parsing.

"Mine, sir," said Conjunction; "it joins the sentences. 'Jack gave a loud cry,' *for* 'lo! a tiger appeared before him.' "

"Lo! lo! lo! that is mine," cried little Interjection, before Serjeant Parsing had time to continue.

"*A*," called out the Serjeant, without noticing him.

"An article, again," said little Article,

"*Tiger*," continued Serjeant Parsing.

"Mine," said Mr. Noun; "a common noun, but nominative this time to the verb *appeared*."

"You should not tell my words, Mr. Noun," said Dr. Verb. "Please, sir, *appeared* is a verb, not active, because it does not say that the tiger appeared to anybody or anything; it appeared *before* somebody, and that little preposi—"

"Now you're telling, Dr. Verb," cried Preposition. "Please, sir, *before* is mine—a preposition, showing the position of the tiger with regard to poor Jack, and governing *him* in the Objective Case; so two marks for me, please, sir."

"One more word," said Serjeant Parsing; "*him*."

"*Him* is mine," said Pronoun, sadly; "it is a personal pronoun, third person and singular number, standing instead of the noun *Jack*;" but, he added, with tears in his eyes, "it is of no use to give me a mark for it, as I shall lose it again on account of the case. *Him* is the objective case, governed by the preposition *before*;" and Pronoun turned away with a sob.

"Well, gentlemen," said Judge Grammar, "you see what the learned Serjeant means by 'parsing.' Only let our Schoolroom Shire friends parse a few sentences in the same way, and they will be perfectly prepared for the great trial that is coming on. Brother, pray hand them up a few." Then pulling out his watch, the Judge continued. "I find, gentlemen, that the present time will soon be past, and we shall be stepping into the future if we go on much longer; therefore I must put off, until the next time we meet, the announcement I was going to make to you today."

The Judge then left the bench, and Serjeant Parsing prepared the following sentences for parsing:

We took a walk in the garden.

I see a bee in your bonnet.

The dragon ate a dragonfly.

You never saw a blue rose.

Ah! I have a bone in my leg.

I will ride behind you on your horse.

Tom picked a flower for me.

Willy is riding on the rocking horse.

A spider has eight legs.

Chapter 17

The Possessive Case; & Who's To Have the Prize?

THE court was again assembled, and the Judge was just going to speak, when he stopped—for there was Mr. Noun, who had gone plop down on one knee before him, just as Dr. Verb did before, and was holding out his petition.

"Dear me," exclaimed the Judge, "you too! What can you have to complain of?"

"I have lost a Case, my lord," said Mr. Noun, still kneeling.

"Get up, sir," said the Judge, "and say out quickly what you mean. Am I never to have done with these tiresome Cases?"

"Please, my lord, it is just this," said Mr. Noun, standing up. "You have seen how my words can be Nominative Case or Objective Case; but there is a case in which they are neither of these two. For instance, in the sentence, 'The monkey pulled the cat's tail,'—*pulled* is the verb; *monkey* is the nominative, for the monkey did the pulling; *tail* is the objective, for 'what did the monkey pull?' The *tail*—but then what case is *cat's*? It is not nominative nor objective."

"Don't ask me what case it is," said the Judge; indignantly; "say out at once yourself."

"But you will be angry at the long word, my lord," said Mr. Noun.

"Nonsense, sir," said the Judge, getting very red. "Speak at once, when I order you to do so."

"Then *cat's* is said to be in the Possessive Case," said Mr. Noun, "because it shows who possessed the tail that was pulled by the monkey. Any noun that shows to whom a thing belongs—who is the possessor of it—is said to be in the Possessive Case."

"Oh!" said the Judge. "Then if I say, 'This knife belongs to Harry,' *Harry* will be in the Possessive Case, will it?"

"No, my lord," said Mr. Noun, looking a little confused, "because there is a little preposition *to* before Harry, and prepositions—"

"Prepositions govern the Objective Case," said Dr. Syntax, solemnly.

"Yes, yes, we know," said Mr. Noun, impatiently; "but I mean any noun that shows possession, without the help of any preposition, as if you said, 'This is Harry's knife.' *Harry's* is in the Possessive Case, for it shows who possesses the knife, not by the help of any preposition, but by making it Harry's instead of *Harry*. I might have said in the other sentence, 'The monkey pulled the tail belonging to the cat,' but it is much better and shorter to use a Possessive Case, and say, 'The monkey pulled the cat's tail.' "

"It certainly seems a convenient case," said the Judge.

"It is, my lord," said Mr. Noun; "and, therefore, I think I have a right to ask for an extra mark for it."

"Oh! that is what you want, is it?" said the Judge. "Well, I might grant your request, provided you can show me an easy way of finding the Possessive Case at once."

"You may always know it by the little apostrophe (') either before or after an s at the end of the word," answered Mr. Noun; "as, 'Mary's doll,' 'Tom's dog,' 'the baby's milk,' 'the children's toys,' 'the boys' hats,' 'the girls' gardens.' Is not that easy, my lord?"

"Yes, that is simple enough," replied the Judge; "therefore, although I think it rather impertinent of you to have brought so many Cases before me, I will grant your request. You are to have then an extra mark for every Nominative Case and for every Possessive Case, but none for the Objective Case; and you will lose a mark every time you are governed by a preposition. Are you satisfied?"

Mr. Noun bowed, and took his seat.

"And now, gentlemen," continued the Judge, addressing the nine Parts-of-Speech, "as you have all appeared before me, and shown clearly who and what you are—"

"And me! oh! oh! poor little me!" cried Interjection.

"I have not called you up before me," said the Judge, sternly, "because we have all heard quite enough about you already. Once is quite enough to have heard such an unruly, odd little creature as you are; and you have thrown yourself in more than once while the people were speaking. We all know that you neither govern nor are governed by any one else, and that you agree with nobody. Therefore, stand aside and be quiet."

"Ah, well!" chuckled Interjection, as he obeyed, "if I do not govern any one, at least I can take my neighbors words, as other people can, and make them my own. Marry! forsooth! indeed! that I can!"

"*Marry* is mine," said Dr. Verb, bustling up.

"Indeed, *indeed* is mine," said Adverb, blandly.

"Pray, do not quarrel with him;" said the Judge; "let him have a few words to keep him quiet."

"There is one thing;" said Dr. Verb, laughing, "no one would be in a hurry to steal Interjection's words, for they are not worth it. Who could ever make a decent word out of *oh*! or *fie*! or *pshaw*! or *ugh*!"

"Laugh as you like, Dr. Verb," cried Interjection, "my words can stand alone, and make sense all by themselves, and mean as much as a whole string of other words. For instance, when I say 'Fie!' that is as good as saying, 'You ought to be ashamed of yourself;' and when I say 'Ah!' that means, 'I see through all your fine airs and graces, Dr. Verb, and know all about you.' Ha! ha! what do you say to that?" And Interjection once more took a turn over head and heels.

"Keep him quiet, will you," said the Judge. "And now, gentlemen; he continued, for the third time, "I hope we shall all be prepared for the great trial that is to take place this day week. The people of Schoolroom Shire are all invited to attend. and to bring their slates and pencils with them. You all, my nine Parts-of-Speech, will together make up a story which Serjeant Parsing will have in his hand. He will then carefully examine every word, and the children of Schoolroom Shire, who will have a place for each of you on their slates, will put down a mark to each one who deserves it. In the end, they will count up all the marks, and the Part-of-Speech who has the most will get—will get—"

Just at this moment, when every one was listening most anxiously to hear what the prize was to be, clouds of dust were observed arising from behind his lordship's throne. In fact, the critics, tired of doing nothing, had begun to turn out whole piles of mouldering old books, Murray's Grammars, old dictionaries, and I know not what; and the venerable dust therefrom, getting into his lordship's eyes, nose, and mouth, brought on such a violent fit of coughing and choking, that it was impossible to get another word from him. He did not then, nor has he since, informed his loving subjects what the prize was to be. Therefore, it is left to the children of Schoolroom Shire to decide. In examining the following story they must be both judge and jury, and decide not only which Part-of-Speech deserves the most marks, but also what is a fitting reward for the happy being who shall win the great prize of Grammar Land.

Serjeant Parsing's Story for the Examination

The Sad Fate of Our Squirrel

Once, when I was walking in the garden, I found a young squirrel on the ground at the foot of a tall tree. It had fallen from the nest. I took the little soft warm creature in my hand, and I carried it carefully into the house. There we fed it with warm milk, and it quickly revived. It soon sat up, with its pretty curly tail over its back, and then it rubbed its nose with its paws. It seemed to look to me as if it knew me for a friend. When night came, I made a soft bed for it beside me, and it slept cosily. In the morning, I took it to my cousin. "It wants breakfast," she said; "I will warm some milk for it in my doll's saucepan." So she boiled some milk in a little green saucepan, and we fed our pet. "Ah!" I cried, "is it ill? It is struggling as if it were in pain." We tried to warm it, and we gave it another spoonful of milk; but, alas! the poor little creature gave a pitiful moan, and we soon saw that it was dead. The green paint on the doll's saucepan was poisonous, and we had killed our little squirrel while it was lying in our arms.

Serjeant Parsing

Grammar Land Worksheets

You may make copies of these worksheets for your personal and family use. Alternatively, you may download and print worksheets on our website blueskydaisies.wordpress.com.

Chapter 1 Worksheet
Mr. Noun

The Judge then spoke "Mr. Noun, you have claimed a great many words, and it remains to be seen whether all the other Parts-of-Speech agree to these words being yours. In order to find out whether they do or no, I will ask our friends from School-room Shire to **write out, each of them, a list of twenty names, the names of anything they can see, hear, touch, taste, smell, or think about, or the proper names of any persons, animals, places, or things they know;** and when next we meet I will read out what they have written, and we shall hear whether any one has any good reason to give why they should not be called nouns."

1. _____

2. _____

3. _____

4. _____

5. _____

6. _____

7. _____

8. _____

9. _____

10. _____

11. _____

12. _____

13. _____

14. _____

15. _____

16. _____

17. _____

18. _____

19. _____

20. _____

Chapter 2 Worksheet
Little Article

"I request that each of you will write six new nouns, and will use an article before every one of them."

List 6 nouns with an article before it.

1. _____
2. _____
3. _____
4. _____
5. _____
6. _____

List 3 nouns with the "an" article before it (nouns that begin with a, e, i, o, and u, or h-mute).

1. _____
2. _____
3. _____

"The court then rose, after Serjeant Parsing had handed the Schoolroom Shire children the following verse, begging them to find out all the nouns and articles in it:

> Once there was a little boy,
>   With curly hair and pleasant eye;
> A boy who always spoke the truth,
>   And never, never told a lie."

List each of the nouns with its article from Serjeant Parsing's verse above.

_____   _____

_____   _____

_____   _____

Chapter 3 Worksheet
Mr. Pronoun

"I will only ask you to assist our Schoolroom Shire friends in making the following verses right. They read very queerly at present; but if you can set them right, I think we shall agree that what you have been saying of your words is true."

The Judge then wished them all good morning, and went to lunch off a few pages of dictionary.

Copy these verses and replace the appropriate nouns with pronouns. In the first two verses, the nouns to replace are underlined.

Here are the verses:

There was a man, <u>the man</u> had no eyes,
And <u>the man</u> went out to view the skies;
<u>The man</u> saw a tree with apples on,
<u>The man</u> took no apples off, and left no apples on.

_____

_____

_____

_____

_____

_____

_____

_____

_____

_____

_____

Little Bo-peep has lost <u>Bo-peep's</u> sheep,
And does not know where to find <u>the sheep</u>;
Leave <u>the sheep</u> alone till <u>the sheep</u> come home,
And bring <u>the sheep's</u> tails behind <u>the sheep</u>.

_____

_____

_____

_____

_____

_____

_____

_____

<u>Underline</u> the appropriate nouns to replace with pronouns and copy the verse below.

Matilda dashed the spectacles away
To wipe Matilda's tingling eyes;
And as in twenty bits the spectacles lay,
Matilda's grandmamma Matilda spies.

_____

_____

_____

_____

_____

_____

_____

_____

_____

Chapter 4 Worksheet
Serjeant Parsing's Visit

"My young friends," he said, in his most amiable voice, "may I trouble you with a little piece of business for Judge Grammar today. I have here a story, and the Judge requests that you will kindly **find out how many of the words in it belong to Mr. Noun, how many to Mr. Pronoun, and how often little ragged Article comes in.** The best way to do this is to get your slates, and mark off a piece for Mr. Noun, another for Mr. Pronoun, and a corner somewhere for little Article. Write their names in each. Now I will read the story, and whenever I come to a noun, give Mr. Noun a mark; whenever I read a pronoun, give a mark to Mr. Pronoun; and if I read an *a, an,* or *the,* put down a mark to little Article. When it is finished we will count up and see who has the most marks."

<u>Underline</u> the nouns, (circle) the pronouns, and draw a [box] around each article. Count the total for each part-of-speech and keep tally marks in the boxes below.

"Some sailors belonging to a ship of war had a monkey on board. The monkey had often watched the men firing off a cannon, so one day when they were all at dinner he thought he should like to fire it too. So he took a match, as he had seen the men do, struck it, put it to the touch hole, and looked into the mouth of the cannon, to see the ball come out. The ball did come out, and alas! alas! the poor little monkey fell down dead."

Noun	Pronoun	Article

Chapter 5 Worksheet
Mr. Adjective

<u>Underline</u> all the adjectives.

THE MAIDEN PRINCE

A long, long time ago, there lived in a grey old castle, a widowed queen, who had one only child, a beautiful bright boy. "My good husband was killed in the terrible war," said the timid queen, "and if my dear son grows up to be a strong man, I fear that he will go to the cruel wars, too, and be killed. So he shall learn nothing about rough war, but shall be brought up like a simple maiden." So she taught him all maidenly duties, to spin, and to weave, and to sew, and she thought he was too simple and quiet to wish to go to war; but one day there came to the great castle gate a noble knight riding a gallant charger. "Come," he cried to the young prince, "come, follow me. I ride to fight with the wicked and strong who are oppressing the weak and the poor." Up sprang, in a moment, the fair young boy, flung aside his girlish work, seized his father's battered sword, and leaped into the saddle behind the noble knight. "Farewell, dear mother," he cried, "no more girlish work for me. I must be a brave man, as my father was, and conquer or die in the rightful cause." Then the foolish queen saw that it was useless to try to make a daring boy into a timid maiden.

Chapter 6 Worksheet
Mr. Adjective Tried for Stealing

"You ought to have known this, Mr. Noun, and not to have accused Mr. Adjective of stealing. Therefore, as a punishment, I require you to send into Schoolroom Shire a list of nouns that may be made into adjectives by the addition of some of Mr. Adjective's tails."

The Judge then left the court, and this is the list that Mr. Noun sent into Schoolroom Shire.

Add the following suffixes to change the noun to the adjective form:

-ful	-less	-like or -ly	-ish
-en	-ern	-y	-ous

1. Truth _____

2. Faith _____

3. Hope _____

4. Care _____

5. Sleep _____

6. Sense _____

7. Lady _____

8. Man _____

9. Love _____

10. Gold _____

11. Wood _____

12. Silk _____

13. Child _____

14. Baby _____

15. Fool _____

16. North _____

17. East _____

18. West _____

19. Dirt _____

20. Wood _____

21. Fire _____

22. Poison _____

23. Danger _____

24. Virtue _____

Chapter 7 Worksheet
The Quarrel between Mr. Adjective & Mr. Pronoun & Little Interjection

Serjeant Parsing then turned to the Schoolroom Shire folks, and asked them to mark off on their slates places for **Mr. Noun, Pronoun, Adjective, and little Article, and a corner somewhere for tiresome Interjection;** and while he read to them, to put down a stroke in the right place for each word that they knew. "And when you come to an adjective-pronoun used with a noun," continued Serjeant Parsing, "put a stroke on the line that divides Adjective's ground from Pronoun's. That will be like a little man sitting astride on the wall, with one leg for Pronoun to pull and one for Adjective. Of course if it is used instead of a noun, and not with one, then Mr. Pronoun must have the stroke all to himself. Whichever Part-of-Speech gets the most strokes gains the game." This is what Serjeant Parsing read.

Label the parts-of-speech in the story on the facing page by marking above each line:

N - Noun	**P - Pronoun**
A - Article	**AdjP - Adjective Pronoun**
Adj - Adjective	**I - Interjection**

Count the total for each part-of-speech and keep tally marks in the boxes.

Noun	Article	Pronoun	Adj Pronoun	Adjective	Interjection

SERJEANT PARSING'S STORY

"Alas! alas! that naughty boy," said Harry's mother, as she waited for him to come back from school. "He must have gone to play with the other boys at the big pond, and he will certainly fall in, for the boys are sure to try the ice, and it is too thin to bear them yet. Oh! my poor, dear boy! what shall I do? If he falls into the black, cold water, he will certainly be drowned. My darling Harry! ah! why does he not come home? If I had any one to send...Why, there he is, I declare, with his hands full of oranges. Oh! the naughty boy! I will give him a great scolding. To give me a fright, and keep me waiting while he was buying oranges! Harry, you are a naughty, careless, tiresome—What! kissing me, you little rogue, to stop my mouth. There! there! do not pull down my hair, and never give your poor mother such a fright again; and now come in and see the lovely Christmas box I have for you."

Chapter 8 Worksheet
Dr. Verb

"Meanwhile, as we shall have further examination of this verb *to be*, I should like my friends in Schoolroom Shire to make a copy of it, to bring with them. I shall also request them to find out all the verbs in the following verses:"

Underline the verbs in each line.

"Sit to your task," a father said,

    "Nor play nor trifle, laugh nor talk,

And when your lesson well is read,

    You all shall have a pleasant walk."

He left the room, the boys sat still,

    Each gravely bent upon his task,

But soon the youngest, little Will,

    Of fun and nonsense chose to ask.

"My ball is lost," the prattler cried,

    "Have either of you seen my ball?"

"Pray mind your book," young Charles replied.

    "Your noisy words disturb us all."

Chapter 9 Worksheet
Dr. Verb's Three Tenses and Number and Person

"That will do, that will do, Dr. Verb," cried the Judge. "We have had your talking in the past tense, we do not want it in the present tense, and if we should happen to require it in the future tense, we will let you know another time. Instead of talking here, you had much better go to Schoolroom Shire, and help the people there to **write out the present, past, and future tenses of the verbs you have mentioned—to have, to live, to sing, to ring**; and show them how the words alter, not only to mark the different times, but to agree with Mr. Pronoun's words in number and person."

In the charts on the following pages, fill in the verb forms for the verbs given, showing their present, past, and future tenses with the correct pronoun.

Fill in the following chart with the verb *to have*.

	Singular	Plural
Present		
1		
2		
3		
Past		
1		
2		
3		
Future		
1		
2		
3		

Fill in the following chart with the verb *to live*.

	Singular	Plural
Present		
1		
2		
3		
Past		
1		
2		
3		
Future		
1		
2		
3		

Fill in the following chart with the verb *to sing*.

	Singular	Plural
Present		
1		
2		
3		
Past		
1		
2		
3		
Future		
1		
2		
3		

Fill in the following chart with the verb *to ring*.

	Singular	Plural
Present		
1		
2		
3		
Past		
1		
2		
3		
Future		
1		
2		
3		

Chapter 10 Worksheet
Serjeant Parsing in Schoolroom Shire Again

"My dear young friends," he said, "will you kindly get your slates, and divide them into four parts, writing at the top of each part, the name of Mr. Noun, Mr. Pronoun, Mr. Adjective, and Dr. Verb. Then cut off two corners somewhere, for little ragged Article and Interjection.

Then listen to the following story, and when any word that you know is read out, give a mark to the Part-of-Speech to whom it belongs. If you come to an adjective-pronoun, of course you must put a little man astride between Mr. Pronoun's ground and Mr. Adjective's; and whenever you come to a verb, please to say whether it is in the present, past, or future tense. When you have done, we will count up, and see which Part-of-Speech has gained the most marks.

For the story "The Two Neighbors" on the facing page, label each part of speech above the word, as follows:

N - Noun	**A - Article**	**P - Pronoun**	**AdjP - Adj Pronoun**
Adj - Adjective	**V - Verb**	**I - Interjection**	

Count the number of each part-of-speech with tally marks in the boxes.

Noun	Article	Pronoun	Adj Pronoun	Adjective	Verb	Interjec-tion

THE TWO NEIGHBORS

A man lived by his labor; and as he had strong arms and a brave heart, he supported, easily, his wife, his little children, and himself.

But a famine came upon the land, and work failed.

The man spent all the money which he had saved, until he had not a penny to buy food for his children.

Then he went to a rich neighbor, and said: "My little children are crying for food, and I have no bread to give them. Help me."

And the rich man said:

"I am a just man; I always pay my debts; but I owe you no money. Go! I cannot give you charity."

Then the poor man went to another neighbor, almost as poor as himself.

"Give me food for my little children," he said.

"Brother," said the poorer neighbor, "we have not much ourselves, but you shall share with us as long as a crust of bread remains."

Then they divided between them the little food that was left, and that food lasted until the hard times had passed.

Chapter 11 Worksheet
The Nominative Case

"Yes," said the Judge; "hand them up, brother. No, do not begin again, Dr. Verb; no more complaints today. And remember, friends, that in these lines every verb must have a Nominative, unless there is a little *to* before the verb. Then it has none—it does not agree with anything. And remember, too, that every noun or pronoun that is in the Nominative case is to get an extra mark on your slates. I wish you good morning, gentlemen."

So saying, the Judge rose. The verses were handed to the people of Schoolroom Shire, and the court was cleared.

Label the nouns with an "N" above the words. Label the pronouns with a "P."
<u>Underline</u> the Nominative Case words. The first line is done for you.

SERJEANT PARSING'S VERSES

     N   **P**   **N**
The <u>hen</u> guards well her little chicks,

The useful cow is meek:

The beaver builds with mud and sticks,

The lapwing loves to squeak.

In Germany they hunt the boar,

The bee brings honey home;

The ant lays up a winter store,

The bear loves honeycomb.

I lost my poor little doll, dears,

As I played on the heath one day;

And I cried for her more than a week, dears,

But I never could find where she lay.

The maidens laughed, the children played,

The boys cut many capers.

While aunt was lecturing the maid,

And uncle read the papers.

Chapter 12 Worksheet
Adverb

I order you to hand up a list of adjectives to be turned into adverbs. Our friends may take them to Schoolroom Shire and put a *-ly* to each of them; then they will be adverbs, and will answer to one of Adverb's questions, how, when, or where."

This is the list Mr. Adjective made out.

For each adjective below, write the adverb form on the blank.

1. quick _____

2. bright _____

3. soft _____

4. strong _____

5. distinct _____

6. clear _____

7. neat _____

8. sharp _____

9. sudden _____

10. late _____

11. punctual _____

12. regular _____

13. sly _____

14. cunning _____

15. false _____

16. true _____

17. pretty _____

18. dainty _____

19. funny _____

20. free _____

21. happy _____

22. awful _____

Chapter 13 Worksheet
Preposition

In spite of the hurry, however, Serjeant Parsing managed to hand up to the people of Schoolroom Shire the following verses, begging the ladies and gentlemen there to find out all the prepositions in them, and to count how many lines there are in which Preposition has nothing to say.

Underline the prepositions. How many lines do not have a preposition? Remember that when *to* comes before a verb, it is not a preposition.

THE FAIRY-RING

<u>Beside</u> a bluebell on the heath,

Among the purple heather,

A fairy lived, and crept beneath

The leaves in windy weather.

She drank the dewdrops from the stalk,

She peeped into the flower;

And then she went to take a walk,

Or ride for half-an-hour.

She rode upon a cricket's back,

She came before the Queen,

The fairy Queen, with all her court,

Within the forest green.

They had a dance upon the grass,

Till larks began to sing;

And where they danced, as all may know

They left a fairy-ring.

Oh, pretty fairies! why not stay,

That we at you may peep?

Why will you only dance and play

When we are fast asleep?

Chapter 14 Worksheet
Prepositions Govern the Objective Case

Serjeant Parsing then took the following lines to Schoolroom Shire, that every Objective Case governed by a preposition might be found out:

> Tom called for me, I went with him,
>   We climbed upon a rock;
> There over the sea we looked for thee,
>   Till seven of the clock.
> And then a white sail over the main,
>   Brought back our sailor-boy again.

Fill in the blanks with a noun or pronoun, and say whether it will be nominative or objective. Be sure to choose a noun or pronoun that agrees with the verb.

_____ went for a walk yesterday,

_____ walked through a dark

_____ under tall _____ ;

suddenly, when _____ were in a very

lonely _____ , _____

heard the steps of some _____ crashing through the

_____ .

    "What can it be?" _____ cried.

_____ stopped to listen; the _____ came

nearer, two bright eyes gleamed at us through the _____ ,

and in another_____ out bounded, with a deep

_____ that made echoes all round us, our own

dear old_____ , who had broken his chain,

escaped from the_____ , and had come

out to look for_____ .

Chapter 15 Worksheet
Conjunction

"Brother Parsing, be good enough to send the following story to Schoolroom Shire, and tell them to give Conjunction a place on their slates among the other Parts-of-Speech, and mark down all his words for him. When that is done, I shall have some good news to tell you."

The court then rose.

<u>Underline</u> all the conjunctions and label the parts of speech above the word, as follows:

N - Noun	P - Pronoun	A - Article
Adj - Adjective	V - Verb	I - Interjection

A NARROW ESCAPE

A traveler in India one day strayed away from his companions, and went to sleep under a tree. When he awoke he saw, to his horror, the two bright eyes of a tiger, ready to spring upon him from a high bank. He leaped up to run away, but fell back again directly, for a large crocodile was coming towards him, with its great mouth open. He shut his eyes and waited in terror, for he heard the tiger spring. A tremendous noise followed; but he felt nothing. He opened his eyes, and lo! the tiger had sprung into the mouth of the crocodile; and while the two wild beasts were struggling, the traveler sprang up and ran away.

Chapter 16 Worksheet
Active Verbs Govern the Objective Case

"Brother Parsing," said the Judge, "let us have a sentence to 'parse,' as you call it, that we may see clearly how it is done."

"Certainly, my lord," said Serjeant Parsing, turning over his papers. "Here is an excellent sentence, or rather, I should say, two sentences, for there are two verbs: 'Jack suddenly gave a loud cry, for lo! a tiger appeared before him.' Now let each Part-of-Speech claim the word as I read it..."

....The Judge then left the bench, and Serjeant Parsing prepared the following sentences for parsing:

Parse these sentences by labeling the parts-of-speech.

1. We took a walk in the garden.

2. I see a bee in your bonnet.

3. The dragon ate a dragonfly.

4. You never saw a blue rose.

5. Ah! I have a bone in my leg.

6. I will ride behind you on your horse.

7. Tom picked a flower for me.

8. Willy is riding on the rocking horse.

9. A spider has eight legs.

Chapter 17 Worksheet
Serjeant Parsing's Story for the Examination

"You all, my nine Parts-of-Speech, will together make up a story which Serjeant Parsing will have in his hand. He will then carefully examine every word, and the children of Schoolroom Shire, who will have a place for each of you on their slates, will put down a mark to each one who deserves it. In the end, they will count up all the marks, and the Part-of-Speech who has the most will get—will get—"

Therefore, it is left to the children of Schoolroom Shire to decide. In examining the following story they must be both judge and jury, and decide not only which Part-of-Speech deserves the most marks, but also what is a fitting reward for the happy being who shall win the great prize of Grammar Land.

Label the parts-of-speech and keep a tally count in the boxes provided.

THE SAD FATE OF OUR SQUIRREL

Once, when I was walking in the garden, I found a young squirrel on the ground at the foot of a tall tree. It had fallen from the nest. I took the little soft warm creature in my hand, and I carried it carefully into the house. There we fed it with warm milk, and it quickly revived. It soon sat up, with its pretty curly tail over its back, and then it rubbed its nose with its paws. It seemed to look to me as if it knew me for a friend. When night came, I made a soft bed for it beside me, and it slept cosily. In the morning, I took it to my cousin. "It wants breakfast," she said; "I will warm some milk for it in my doll's saucepan." So she boiled some milk in a little green saucepan, and we fed our pet. "Ah!" I cried, "is it ill? It is struggling as if it were in pain." We tried to warm it, and we gave it another spoonful of milk; but, alas! the poor little creature gave a pitiful moan, and we soon saw that it was dead. The green paint on the doll's saucepan was poisonous, and we had killed our little squirrel while it was lying in our arms.

Noun	Pronoun	Article	Adjective	Verb	Adverb

Preposition	Conjunction	Interjection

Answer Key

Chapter 1 - Mr. Noun

Students should list any 20 nouns.

For example: dog, cat, house, barn, song, bench, mom, school, crackers, towel, purse, beach, smoothie, flower, restaurant, book, orange, butterfly, grass, toy

Chapter 2 - Little Article

Students should first list six nouns with an article (*a* or *the*) before the noun, then three with the article *an* before it. For example: **a** tree, **the** mountain, **a** desk, **the** brain; and then: **an** ice cream cone, **an** elephant, **an** heir.

Students should find six nouns from Serjeant Parsing's verse: a boy, hair, eye, a boy, the truth, a lie.

Chapter 3 - Mr. Pronoun

Changes shown in **(parenthesis).**

There was a man, ~~the man~~ **(who)** had no eyes,
And ~~the man~~ **(he)** went out to view the skies;
~~The man~~ **(He)** saw a tree with apples on,
~~The man~~ **(He)** took no apples off, and left no apples on.

Little Bo-peep has lost ~~Bo-peep's~~ **(her)** sheep,
And does not know where to find ~~the sheep~~ **(them)**;
Leave ~~the sheep~~ **(them)** alone till ~~the sheep~~ **(they)** come home,
And bring ~~the sheep's~~ **(their)** tails behind ~~the sheep~~ **(them)**.

Matilda dashed the spectacles away
To wipe ~~Matilda's~~ **(her)** tingling eyes;
And as in twenty bits ~~the spectacles~~ **(they)** lay,
Matilda's grandmamma ~~Matilda~~ **(she)** spies.

Chapter 4 - Serjeant Parsing's Visit

Students were asked to underline nouns, draw a circle around pronouns, and draw a box around articles. Nouns are underlined in the key, pronouns are circled, and articles are shown in bold face.

"Some <u>sailors</u> belonging to **a** <u>ship of war</u> had **a** <u>monkey</u> on <u>board</u>. **The** <u>monkey</u> had often watched **the** <u>men</u> firing off **a** <u>cannon</u>, so one <u>day</u> when (they) were all at <u>dinner</u> (he) thought (he) should like to fire (it) too. So (he) took **a** <u>match</u>, as (he) had seen **the** <u>men</u> do, struck (it) put (it) to **the** <u>touch hole</u>, and looked into **the** <u>mouth</u> of **the** <u>cannon</u>, to see **the** <u>ball</u> come out. **The** <u>ball</u> did come out, and alas! alas! **the** poor little <u>monkey</u> fell down dead."

Noun	Pronoun	Article
## ## ## ## II 17	## III 8	## ## III 13

Note: "Ship of war" is a warship. "Touch hole" refers to the hole near the rear of a cannon where ignition occurs.

Chapter 5 - Mr. Adjective

Adjectives are underlined.

A <u>long</u>, <u>long</u> time ago, there lived in a <u>grey</u> <u>old</u> castle, a <u>widowed</u> queen, who had <u>one</u> <u>only</u> child, a <u>beautiful</u> <u>bright</u> boy. "My <u>good</u> husband was killed in the <u>terrible</u> war," said the <u>timid</u> queen, "and if my <u>dear</u> son grows up to be a <u>strong</u> man, I fear that he will go to the <u>cruel</u> wars, too, and be killed. So he shall learn nothing about <u>rough</u> war, but shall be brought up like a <u>simple</u> maiden." So she taught him <u>all</u> <u>maidenly</u> duties, to spin, and to weave, and to sew, and she thought he was too <u>simple</u> and <u>quiet</u> to wish to go to war; but <u>one</u> day there came to the <u>great</u> <u>castle</u> gate a <u>noble</u> knight riding a <u>gallant</u> charger. "Come," he cried to the <u>young</u> prince, "come, follow me. I ride to fight with the wicked and strong who are oppressing the weak and the poor." Up sprang, in a moment, the <u>fair</u> <u>young</u> boy, flung aside his <u>girlish</u> work, seized his <u>father's</u> <u>battered</u> sword, and leaped into the saddle behind the <u>noble</u> knight. "Farewell, <u>dear</u> mother," he cried, "no more <u>girlish</u> work for me. I must be a <u>brave</u> man, as my father was, and conquer or die in the <u>rightful</u> cause." Then the <u>foolish</u> queen saw that it was useless to try to make a <u>daring</u> boy into a <u>timid</u> maiden.

Note: *Simple* and *quiet* are predicate adjectives in this instance. Your student may forget to underline them as adjectives.

Chapter 6 - Mr. Adjective Tried for Stealing

Students were asked to add the following suffixes to form adjectives (some nouns have more than one possibility):

-ful	-less	-like or -ly	-ish
-en	-ern	-y	-ous

1. truthful
2. faithful, faithless
3. hopeful, hopeless
4. careful, careless
5. sleepy, sleepless
6. senseless, sensous
7. ladylike
8. manly
9. lovely
10. golden
11. wooden, woody
12. silken, silky
13. childless, childlike, childish
14. babyish, babylike
15. foolish
16. Northern
17. Eastern
18. Western
19. dirty
20. wooden, woody
21. fiery (note spelling change)
22. poisonous
23. dangerous
24. virtuous

Chapter 7 - The Quarrel between Mr. Adjective & Mr. Pronoun & Little Interjection

Students were instructed to label the parts-of-speech by marking above each line:
Noun - N, Article - A, Pronoun - P, Adj-Pronoun- AdjP, Adjective - Adj, Interj - I

Noun	Article	Pronoun	Adj Pronoun	Adjective	Interjection
⦀⦀⦀⦀⦀	⦀⦀⦀	⦀⦀⦀⦀⦀	⦀⦀	⦀⦀⦀⦀	⦀⦀
25	11	23	7	21	10

 I   I   AdjP   Adj   N   Adj*   N   P   P
"Alas! alas! that naughty boy," said Harry's mother, as she waited for him

         N   P   A   Adj   N
to come back from school. "He must have gone to play with the other boys at

A Adj   N   P   A   N   A   N
the big pond, and he will certainly fall in, for the boys are sure to try the ice,

   P   Adj   P   I AdjP Adj   Adj   N   P   P
and it is too thin to bear them yet. Oh! my poor, dear boy! what shall I do? If

P   A   Adj   Adj   N   P   AdjP Adj
he falls into the black, cold water, he will certainly be drowned. My darling

N   I   P   N   P   Adj   N   I   Adj
Harry! ah! why does he not come home? If I had any one to send...Why, there

P   (------ I ------)   AdjP   N   N   I   A   Adj   N   P
he is, I declare, with his hands full of oranges. Oh! the naughty boy! I will give

P   A   Adj   N   P   A   N   P   P
him a great scolding. To give me a fright, and keep me waiting while he was

        N   N   P   A   Adj   Adj   Adj   I
buying oranges! Harry, you are a naughty, careless, tiresome—What! kissing

P   P   Adj   N   AdjP   N   I   I   AdjP   N
me, you little rogue, to stop my mouth. There! there! do not pull down my hair,

        AdjP Adj   N   A   N
and never give your poor mother such a fright again; and now come in and

    A   Adj   Adj   N   P   P
see the lovely Christmas box I have for you."

Note: *Harry's is technically a possessive modifier (adjective), but since Harry is a proper noun, your student might label it as a noun. We are counting it as an adjective. I declare is labeled as an interjection, because this phrase is serving as an expression of emotion by the speaker, thrown in the middle of the sentence.

Chapter 8 - Dr. Verb

Underline the verbs for each line.

"<u>Sit</u> to your task," a father <u>said</u>,

   "Nor <u>play</u> nor <u>trifle</u>, <u>laugh</u> nor <u>talk</u>,

And when your lesson well <u>is</u> <u>read</u>,

   You all <u>shall</u> <u>have</u> a pleasant walk."

He <u>left</u> the room, the boys <u>sat</u> still,

   Each gravely <u>bent</u> upon his task,

But soon the youngest, little Will,

   Of fun and nonsense <u>chose</u> to <u>ask</u>.

"My ball <u>is</u> lost," the prattler <u>cried</u>,

   "<u>Have</u> either of you <u>seen</u> my ball?"

"Pray <u>mind</u> your book," young Charles <u>replied</u>.

   "Your noisy words <u>disturb</u> us all."

Note: "Pray" in the sentence, "Pray mind your book," is used as a preface to a polite instruction, similarly to please. It serves as an adverb in this circumstance, not a verb.

Chapter 9 - Dr. Verb's Three Tenses and Number and Person

Fill in the following chart with the verb *to have*.

		Singular	Plural
		Present	
1		I have	We have
2		You have	You (pl) have
3		He, She, It has	They have
		Past	
1		I had	We had
2		You had	You (pl) had
3		He, She, It had	They had
		Future	
1		I will have	We will have
2		You will have	You (pl) will have
3		He, She, It will have	They will have

Fill in the following chart with the verb *to live*.

		Singular	Plural
		Present	
1		I live	We live
2		You live	You (pl) live
3		He, She, It lives	They live
		Past	
1		I lived	We lived
2		You lived	You (pl) lived
3		He, She, It lived	They lived
		Future	
1		I will live	We will live
2		You will live	You (pl) will live
3		He, She, It will live	They will live

Fill in the following chart with the verb *to sing*.

	Singular	Plural
	Present	
1	I sing	We sing
2	You sing	You (pl) sing
3	He, She, It sings	They sing
	Past	
1	I sang	We sang
2	You sang	You (pl) sang
3	He, She, It sang	They sang
	Future	
1	I will sing	We will sing
2	You will sing	You (pl) will sing
3	He, She, It will sing	They will sing

Fill in the following chart with the verb *to ring*.

	Singular	Plural
	Present	
1	I ring	We ring
2	You ring	You (pl) ring
3	He, She, It rings	They ring
	Past	
1	I rang	We rang
2	You rang	You (pl) rang
3	He, She, It rang	They rang
	Future	
1	I will ring	We will ring
2	You will ring	You (pl) will ring
3	He, She, It will ring	They will ring

Chapter 10 – Serjeant Parsing in Schoolroom Shire Again

THE TWO NEIGHBORS

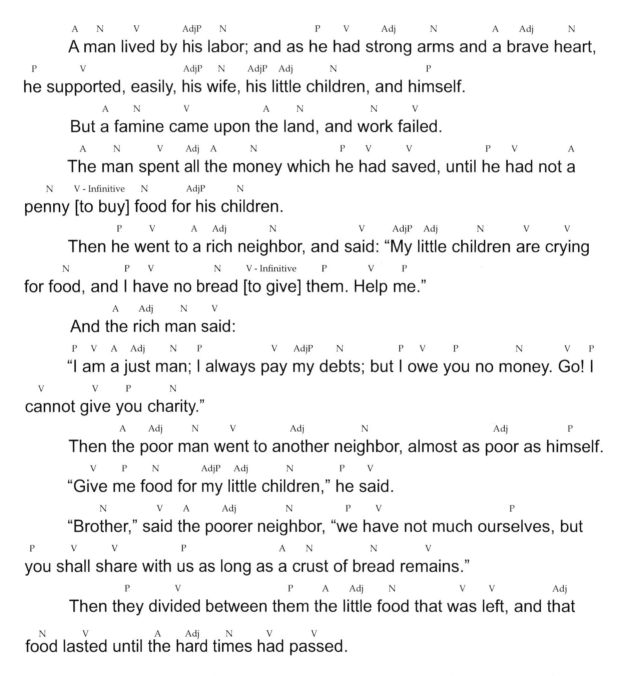

A man lived by his labor; and as he had strong arms and a brave heart, he supported, easily, his wife, his little children, and himself.

But a famine came upon the land, and work failed.

The man spent all the money which he had saved, until he had not a penny [to buy] food for his children.

Then he went to a rich neighbor, and said: "My little children are crying for food, and I have no bread [to give] them. Help me."

And the rich man said:

"I am a just man; I always pay my debts; but I owe you no money. Go! I cannot give you charity."

Then the poor man went to another neighbor, almost as poor as himself.

"Give me food for my little children," he said.

"Brother," said the poorer neighbor, "we have not much ourselves, but you shall share with us as long as a crust of bread remains."

Then they divided between them the little food that was left, and that food lasted until the hard times had passed.

Note: Although "Go!" is a short exclamation that might seem to be an interjection, it is in fact an imperative command and not merely an expression of emotion thrown in, as interjections are. See chapter 7 for help understanding interjections.

For the story "The Two Neighbors" on the previous page (shown with the answers), students were instructed to label each part of speech above the word, as follows:

N - Noun	A - Article	P - Pronoun	AdjP - Adj Pronoun
Adj - Adjective	V - Verb	I - Interjection	

They were also instructed to count the number of each part-of-speech with tally marks in the boxes. The boxes are filled in below.

Noun	Article	Pronoun	Adj Pronoun	Adjective	Verb	Interjection
卌 卌 卌 卌 卌 卌 IIII 34	卌 卌 卌 15	卌 卌 卌 卌 IIII 24	卌 III 7	卌 卌 卌 I 16	卌 卌 卌 卌 卌 卌 卌 III 38	

Students were instructed to say what tense the verbs were:

lived - past
had - past
supported - past
came - past
failed - past
spent - past
had saved - past
had - past
went - past
said - past
are crying - present progressive
have - present
help - present
said - past
am - present

pay - present
owe - present
Go - present
can give - present
went - past
give - present
said - past
said - past
have - present
shall share - future
remains - present
divided - past
was left - passive past
lasted - past tense
had passed - past perfect

Note: Possessive pronouns are marked as AdjP (adjective pronouns) and counted in the Adjective Pronoun tally box. Infinitive verbs are marked for you and counted as verbs.

Chapter 11 – The Nominative Case

Nouns should be labeled with an "N," pronouns with a "P," and nominative case nouns or pronouns should be underlined.

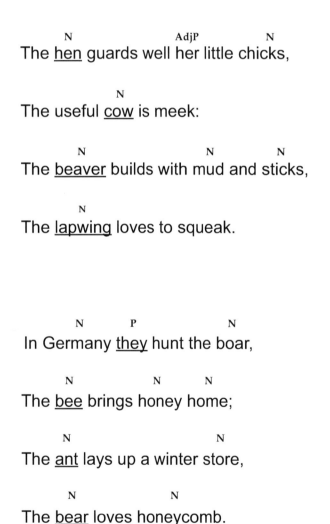

      N   AdjP   N
The <u>hen</u> guards well her little chicks,

          N
The useful <u>cow</u> is meek:

    N   N   N
The <u>beaver</u> builds with mud and sticks,

    N
The <u>lapwing</u> loves to squeak.

   N   P   N
In Germany <u>they</u> hunt the boar,

  N   N   N
The <u>bee</u> brings honey home;

  N   N
The <u>ant</u> lays up a winter store,

  N   N
The <u>bear</u> loves honeycomb.

Note: In line 2, "The useful cow is meek," "meek" is a predicate adjective, describing "cow."

P   AdjP   N   N
I lost my poor little doll, dears,

P   N   N
As I played on the heath one day;

P   P   N   N
And I cried for her more than a week, dears,

P   P
But I never could find where she lay.

N   N
The maidens laughed, the children played,

N   N
The boys cut many capers.

N   N
While aunt was lecturing the maid,

N   N
And uncle read the papers.

Chapter 12 - Adverb

1. quick: *quickly*
2. bright: *brightly*
3. soft: *softly*
4. strong: *strongly*
5. distinct: *distinctly*
6. clear: *clearly*
7. neat: *neatly*
8. sharp: *sharply*
9. sudden: *suddenly*
10. late: *lately*
11. punctual: *punctually*
12. regular: *regularly*
13. sly: *slyly*
14. cunning: *cunningly*
15. false: *falsely*
16. true: *truly*
17. pretty: *prettily*
18. dainty: *daintily*
19. funny: *funnily*
20. free: *freely*
21. happy: *happily*
22. awful: *awfully*

Chapter 13 - Preposition

Prepositions are underlined below. There are 15 prepositions in the poem. Six lines do not have a preposition.

Beside a bluebell on the heath,
   Among the purple heather,
A fairy lived, and crept beneath
   The leaves in windy weather.

She drank the dewdrops from the stalk,
   She peeped into the flower;
And then she went to take a walk,
   Or ride for half-an-hour.

She rode upon a cricket's back,
   She came before the Queen,
The fairy Queen, with all her court,
   Within the forest green.

They had a dance upon the grass,
   Till larks began to sing;
And where they danced, as all may know
   They left a fairy-ring.

Oh, pretty fairies! why not stay,
   That we at you may peep?
Why will you only dance and play
   When we are fast asleep?

Note: The "to" used as an infinitive with a verb is not a preposition in that usage. Therefore "to take" and "to sing" are not prepositions.

Chapter 14 - Prepositions Govern the Objective Case

Fill in the blanks with a noun or pronoun, and say whether it will be nominative or objective. Answers vary; possible answers shown.

_____George and I (nominative)_____ went for a walk yesterday. _____We (nominative)_____ walked through a dark _____forest (objective)_____ under tall _____trees (objective)_____ ; suddenly, when _____we (nominative)_____ were in a very lonely _____clearing (objective)_____ , _____we (nominative)_____ heard the steps of some _____animal (objective)_____ crashing through the _____trees (objective)_____ .

"What can it be?" _____I (nominative)_____ cried.

_____George (nominative) stopped to listen; the _____animal (nominative)_____ came nearer, two bright eyes gleamed at us through the _____leaves (objective),_____ and in another_____minute (objective)_____ out bounded, with a deep _____howl (objective)_____ that made echoes all round us, our own dear old_____dog (nominative)_____ , who had broken his chain, escaped from the_____leash (objective)_____ , and had come out to look for_____us (objective)_____ .

Chapter 15 - Conjunction

A NARROW ESCAPE

A   N   Prep N   Adj   N   V   Adv   Prep AdjP   N   C

A traveler in India one day strayed away from his companions, <u>and</u>

V   V - Infinitive   Prep A N   Adv   P   V   P   V   Prep AdjP   N   A   Adj

went [to sleep] under a tree. When he awoke he saw, to his horror, the two

Adj   N   Prep A   N   Adj   V - Infinitive   Prep   P   Prep A Adj   N   P   V

bright eyes of a tiger, ready [to spring] upon him from a high bank. He leaped

Adv V-Infinitive   Adv   C   V   Adv   Adv   Adv   C A Adj   N   V   V

up [to run] away, <u>but</u> fell back again directly, <u>for</u> a large crocodile was coming

Prep   P   Prep AdjP Adj   N   Adj   P   V AdjP N   C   V Prep N

towards him, with its great mouth open. He shut his eyes <u>and</u> waited in terror,

C   P   V   A   N   V   A   Adj   N   V   C   P   V   N

<u>for</u> he heard the tiger spring. A tremendous noise followed; <u>but</u> he felt nothing.

P   V   AdjP N   C   I   A   N   V   V   Prep A   N   Prep A

He opened his eyes, <u>and</u> lo! the tiger had sprung into the mouth of the

N   C   Adv   A Adj Adj   N   V   V   A   N   V

crocodile; <u>and</u> while the two wild beasts were struggling, the traveler sprang

Adv   C   V   Adv

up <u>and</u> ran away.

Note: Students were asked to underline conjunctions and label nouns, pronouns, adjectives, articles, verbs, and interjections. We have also labeled prepositions and adverbs above for your clarification. Additionally, we have identified possessive pronouns as adjective pronouns.

Chapter 16 - Active Verbs Govern the Objective Case

    P   V   A   N   Prep A   N
1. We took a walk in the garden.

    P V   A   N   Prep AdjP   N
2. I see a bee in your bonnet.

    A   N   V   A   N
3. The dragon ate a dragonfly.

    P   Adv   V   A Adj   N
4. You never saw a blue rose.

   I   P   V   A   N   Prep AdjP N
5. Ah! I have a bone in my leg.

    P   V   V   Prep   P   Prep AdjP   N
6. I will ride behind you on your horse.

    N   V   A   N   Prep   P
7. Tom picked a flower for me.

    N   V   V   Prep A   Adj   N
8. Willy is riding on the rocking horse.

    A   N   V   Adj   N
9. A spider has eight legs.

Chapter 17 - Sergeant Parsing's Story for the Examination

THE SAD FATE OF OUR SQUIRREL

Adv   C   P   V   V   Prep A   N   P V A Adj   N   Prep A
Once, when I was walking in the garden, I found a young squirrel on the

N   Prep A   N   Prep A Adj   N   P V   V   Prep   A   N   P V A Adj Adj
ground at the foot of a tall tree. It had fallen from the nest. I took the little soft

Adj   N   Prep P   N   C P   V   P   Adv   Prep A   N   Adv   P
warm creature in my hand, and I carried it carefully into the house. There we

V P Prep Adj   N   C P   Adv   V   P Adv   V Adv Prep AdjP Adj   Adj
fed it with warm milk, and it quickly revived. It soon sat up, with its pretty curly

N   Prep AdjP N   C   Adv P V   AdjP N   Prep AdjP N   P   V   V - Infinitive
tail over its back, and then it rubbed its nose with its paws. It seemed [to look]

Prep P C C P   V   P   Prep A   N   C   N   V P V   A Adj   N   Prep P
to me as if it knew me for a friend. When night came, I made a soft bed for it

Prep   P   C   P   V   Adv   Prep A   N   P   V P Prep AdjP   N   P   V
beside me, and it slept cosily. In the morning, I took it to my cousin. "It wants

N   P   V   P V   V   Adj   N Prep P Prep AdjP Adj   N   C
breakfast," she said, "I will warm some milk for it in my doll's saucepan." So

P   V   Adj   N   Prep A Adj   Adj   N   C   P   V P N   I   P
she boiled some milk in a little green saucepan, and we fed our pet. "Ah!" I

V   V P Adj   P V   V   C C P   V   Prep N   P   V   V - Infinitive   P   C
cried, "is it ill? It is struggling as if it were in pain." We tried [to warm] it, and

P   V   P   Adj   N   Prep N   C   I   A   Adj   Adj   N   V   A
we gave it another spoonful of milk; but, alas! the poor little creature gave a

Adj   N   C   P   Adv   V   C P   V   N   A   Adj   N   Prep A Adj
pitiful moan, and we soon saw that it was dead. The green paint on the doll's

N   V   Adj   C P   V   V   AdjP Adj   N   C   P   V
saucepan was poisonous, and we had killed our little squirrel while it was

V Prep AdjP   N
lying in our arms.

Noun	Pronoun	Article	Adjective	Verb	Adverb
卌 卌 卌 卌 卌 卌 卌 35	卌 卌 卌 卌 卌 卌 卌 卌 卌 IIII 49	卌 卌 I 16	卌 卌 卌 卌 III 23	卌 卌 卌 卌 卌 卌 卌 卌 40	卌 IIII 9

Preposition	Conjunction	Interjection
卌 卌 卌 卌 IIII 24	卌 卌 卌 III 18	II 2

Note: Footnote from Chapter 15, page 149, applies to this worksheet as well. Additionally, we have identified possessive pronouns as adjective pronouns. The student's tally marks can count these as pronouns.

Subordinating conjunctions introducing adverbial clauses are labeled as conjunctions. Students could mistake these for adverbs.

Made in the USA
Columbia, SC
13 October 2022

69395368R00085